The Product Manager Powerhouse

Become a Stronger PM

Written by Liam Hawking

Published by Cornell-David Publishing House

Index

Chapter 1:

1.1 The Evolving Role of the Product Manager

Picture this scenario: You're a product manager in the 1990's for a growing software company. Life is simple; your role consists primarily of gathering requirements from users and stakeholders, writing detailed documentation to pass along to the development team, and make sure the product is developed as planned.

Flash forward to today, and you might be a little shocked. The role of the product manager has undergone a significant transformation, following the pace at which technology and ideas are changing in the world. As Benedict Studios aptly puts it, "New ideas and new products appear and disappear at a speed that 25 years ago would have been unimaginable" (Eisenstein, 2016). The role of the product manager today is hardly recognizable from what it used to be, and the demands of the job have expanded exponentially (Johansson-Söderstjerna & Hellström, 2017).

Let's break it down and look at the key aspects that define the role of product managers in this ever-evolving industry.

Strategic Thinker: The product manager of today has to think strategically and be involved in shaping the product vision, as well as defining its value proposition. This means that product managers must go beyond simply handing off specifications - it's now their job to create a compelling story that makes customers want to use the product. As such, they must possess strong analytical capabilities to identify trends in the market, set the direction for the product, and help the organisation make forward-looking decisions.

Technological Savvy: In the era of digital transformation, product managers can no longer afford to simply rely on their business acumen to deliver successful products. They need to be familiar with emerging technologies and understand how these can be leveraged to create a competitive advantage. Specifically, they must appreciate data-driven decision-making and adopt a hypothesis-driven approach to product management (Johnston, 2018).

Cross-functional expertise: The lines between roles in product development are becoming increasingly blurred. Today's product managers must collaborate with various teams, including engineering, design, marketing, sales, and customer support. They must lead by example and be effective communicators to facilitate problem-solving across teams, create transparency in operations, and enable the development of better solutions.

Consumer-centric: One of the most important ways in which the role of the product manager has evolved is their focus on the end consumer. They must now empathize with the user's pain points, develop solutions that truly address their needs, and validate their assumptions through user research and testing. This user-centered mindset is more important than ever, as it drives deeper engagement and higher lifetime value for the product.

Now that we've established the key facets that characterize a modern product manager let's examine the practical advice that'll help you succeed in this rapidly evolving industry.

Deep Insight #1: Focus on continuously learning and upskilling
As the role of the product manager is constantly evolving, so must your skillset. According to a research study by Johansson-Söderstjerna & Hellström (2017), "continuous learning and personal transformation are key to ensuring that product managers remain relevant in the industry".

For this reason, it's crucial that you stay up-to-date with technological advancements, changing market and user requirements, and new methodologies and frameworks that may impact product management. Whether it be through online courses, workshops, or joining product management communities, always find ways to propel learning and professional growth.

Deep Insight #2: Cultivate your digital quotient
To thrive as a product manager in today's digitally driven business landscape, you need to cultivate what Forrester Research calls "digital intelligence," a term that reflects the combination of analytical and creative talents required to build successful digital products. Focusing on visual and data storytelling can help you effectively communicate product vision and strategy to various stakeholders, from engineering to marketing.

Moreover, developing data literacy allows you to harness the power of data in driving product decisions, measure progress against key goals, and make course changes when needed. Implementing hypothesis-driven product management can help create a more agile, data-driven culture within the company.

In conclusion, the role of the product manager has come a long way since its strict requirement gathering days. Today's product managers must develop a powerful blend of strategic thinking, technological savvy, cross-functional expertise, and customer-centricity to successfully navigate the complex ecosystem of modern product management. By focusing on continuous learning and cultivating digital intelligence, product managers can stay ahead of the curve and deliver best-in-class products that create lasting value for their users and companies alike.

1.2 Core competencies and skills for success

I cannot emphasize enough the importance of developing core competencies and skills for success in this domain. Product management is an ever-evolving field, and the challenges of this job constantly fluctuate due to growing demands of customers, rapid technological advancements, and increasing competitive pressures. Consequently, it is crucial for product managers (PMs) to be well-rounded individuals who know their product like the back of their hand and can strategize, execute, and deliver efficiently. In this section, we will dive into the essential competencies that product managers need to develop, highlighting relevant research and insights to support your journey in becoming a stronger product manager.

Technical proficiency: Often seen as the backbone of a successful product manager, technical proficiency is critical in understanding your product, addressing potential problems, and making informed decisions. A study conducted by Cagan (2008) found that having a technical background is a strong foundation for product managers as it enables them to understand the underlying systems and speak the same language as software engineers, thus resulting in better collaboration. However, do remember that while technical proficiency is important, it should not overshadow the significance of other core competencies.

Market and customer knowledge: A stellar product manager needs to have an in-depth understanding of their target customers and the market landscape. According to a research study by Huang and Lai (2011), PMs with a profound understanding of customer needs and market trends can create better strategies and make informed decisions, which subsequently lead to product success. To systematically acquire this knowledge, immerse yourself in customer feedback, conduct surveys and interviews, attend conferences and webinars, and follow industry news and influencers to stay informed.

Data-driven decision-making: In today's data-centric world, a successful product manager must harness data effectively to make informed decisions. This skill involves understanding the data available, drawing relevant insights, and leveraging it to optimize your product strategy. Always ensure you assess data from a range of sources (user feedback, market trends, competitor analysis, and product performance) and tell compelling stories with data to guide your team and stakeholders (Perry, 2015).

Strategic thinking: Strong PMs are visionaries who can see the bigger picture; they possess the ability to identify opportunities and threats through a long-term lens. This skill entails assessing competitive threats, analyzing trends, anticipating changes, and adjusting goals and objectives accordingly. As cited by Alexander Osterwalder, a renowned author and consultant, "a great product manager has the brain of an engineer, the heart of a designer, and the speech of a diplomat." Thus, you need to balance analytical skills and intuition to efficiently strategize, prioritize, and manage valuable resources (Osterwalder, 2011).

Effective communication: As a product manager, you will be the central hub for your product, liaising with various teams, stakeholders, and customers. Therefore, the ability to communicate effectively is indispensable. Mastering the art of active listening, clear writing, persuasive speaking, and empathetic exchange can propel your ability to collaborate and lead your team to product success. A study by Katzell and Thompson (1990) highlighted the positive correlation between effective communication and better team performance, a reciprocity that is essential for PMs.

Deep Insight 1: It is important to note, however, that excelling in these core competencies is a constantly evolving process. To keep up with the dynamic nature of the product management landscape, it's essential to adopt a growth mindset, where you view your abilities as continually enhancing through dedicated efforts, open-mindedness, and embracing challenges (Dweck, 2006). This mindset will not only help you develop your skills consistently but also adapt to the ever-changing demands of product management.

Deep Insight 2: The perfect blend of soft skills and hard skills will maximize your potential as a product manager. While traditional hard skills such as technical proficiency, data analytics, and strategic thinking provide a solid foundation for PMs, it is often the soft skills, like communication, empathy, and adaptability that can be the differentiating factor to drive product success. Hence, the key takeaway is to strike a balance between both these skill sets, perpetually honing and improving them.

In conclusion, developing core competencies and skills is crucial to becoming a stronger product manager. Focus on honing your technical proficiency, market and customer knowledge, data-driven decision-making, strategic thinking, and effective communication skills. Remember that there is always room for growth and improvement, so keep learning and adapting to become the best product manager you can be.

1.3 Building and Leading Cross-Functional Teams

I've observed that one of the most critical skills required to become a stronger product manager is the ability to build and lead cross-functional teams. Cross-functional teams are diverse groups of individuals with specialized skills and expertise who collaborate to deliver value and achieve a shared vision (Fisher, 2019). In today's fast-paced and competitive business environment, organizations rely on these collaborative teams to drive innovation and tackle the complex challenges they face. This section of the book will address the importance of building and leading these teams effectively and offer practical advice for your product management journey.

To be successful at building cross-functional teams, you must begin with a strong foundation, and that includes attracting and selecting the right people. Each team member should bring their technical skills and unique experiences to ensure a diverse range of perspectives (Gratton & Erickson, 2007). While hiring new employees, it's essential to prioritize diversity in terms of skills, thought, opinions, and backgrounds. Not only these diverse teams result in more creative solutions, but the decisions made by them are also better informed (Phillips, 2014).

As you assemble your team, remember to take a close look at the team's culture and dynamics. Foster an environment where team members feel comfortable to share their ideas, critiques, and perspectives. Also, pay attention to the personality types that work best within the group, understanding that strong teams need balance. For instance, having too many forceful and outspoken team members may hinder deeper conversations, whereas having too many introverted members may limit the sharing of valuable ideas.

One deep insight for building successful cross-functional teams is to ensure clear communication and a shared understanding of the team's objectives. It is vital to establish a common language and communication style that everyone can understand and use effectively. As a product manager, you should lead by example, encouraging everyone to express their views, ask questions, and constructively challenge one another. With open and transparent communication, you can create an environment of trust, making collaboration and innovation more accessible.

Another deep insight is to set clear expectations and roles for each team member while embracing the flexibility to adapt as needed. Be proactive in assigning responsibilities and establishing how decisions will be made. Additionally, ensure that the team members understand the purpose of their roles within the team and how they contribute to the overall vision. This clarity will help reduce potential conflicts and improve overall productivity.

Leading cross-functional teams is no easy task, as you must manage a diverse group of people with varying perspectives and expectations. Be open to learning from your team and seek to understand each member's motivation, priorities, and goals. Consider adopting a servant leadership approach where your focus is on empowering and developing the team members rather than solely driving the team's output. Studies have shown that this leadership style positively impacts team performance and engagement (Liden, Wayne, Meuser, 2014).

To lead, motivate, and collaborate effectively, invest time in building strong relationships with each team member. This collaborative leadership approach not only helps in increasing trust but also in becoming a better leader. Remember that growth is a continuous journey and teams evolve over time as their projects advance or change tracks (Dubinski, 2016). Be flexible and adaptable while understanding various dynamics, strengths, and weaknesses to ensure that your team remains cohesive and responsive to your leadership.

In conclusion, building and leading cross-functional teams are essential skills for product managers to master. By focusing on diversity, ensuring clear communication, setting expectations, and adopting a servant leadership approach, you will be well-equipped to manage these teams effectively. These teams can drive significant value and innovation for your organization, helping you become a stronger product manager in the process. Always remember that successful product management starts with a powerful, dynamic, and collaborative team behind it.

1.4 Developing A Customer-Centric Mindset

I cannot emphasize enough the importance of developing a customer-centric mindset. In this section, we'll dive deep into understanding why customer-centricity is crucial and discuss practical tips for fostering such a mindset. Keep in mind that putting your customers' needs first is not only a sound business strategy but also a way to enable long-lasting success for your products, your team, and your company.

Why is a customer-centric mindset crucial in product management?

First and foremost, let's discuss why it's essential to develop a customer-centric mindset in the world of product management. A study by Deloitte and Touche, cited by Harvard Business Review, found that customer-centric companies are 60% more profitable than those that aren't (Rogers & Tanner, 2017). Furthermore, a report by PwC found that 73% of consumers say a good experience is instrumental in influencing their brand loyalties (PwC, 2018). These findings indicate that a customer-centric approach can significantly impact your company's bottom line and overall success.

So, how do you go about developing this mindset? The key is to empathize with your customers, understand their needs, and create the best possible user experience. Here are some practical ways to achieve this:

1. Understand your customers' personas and their pain points.

Before diving into product development, you need first to understand your target audience deeply. Create data-driven customer personas that reflect the different segments of your market. Then, focus on uncovering and addressing their specific pain points (Schneider & Hall, 2011). This will not only help you develop targeted solutions, but it will also facilitate a deeper connection with your customers.

Tip: *Practice empathy mapping* by putting yourself in your customer's shoes and considering their thoughts, feelings, and frustrations. This exercise will help you identify gaps in your product's user experience and inform your decision-making process.

2. Centralize decision-making around the customer's needs.

As a product manager, always ask yourself, "How does this decision benefit the customer?" Ensure your team members prioritize customer-centric thinking in every step of the development process. By making the customer the focal point of your decisions, you'll create a positive user experience that directly addresses their needs and desires.

Tip: *Consistently ask for customer feedback* and involve them in your decision-making process through focus groups, surveys, or one-on-one interviews. This practice will ensure your customers feel heard and valued, and it will keep your product aligned with their expectations and requirements.

3.Evaluate your product's success based on customer satisfaction metrics.

To truly adopt a customer-centric mindset, you need to shift your definition of product success to center on customer satisfaction. Invest in measuring customer satisfaction through quantitative methods, such as Net Promoter Score (NPS) or Customer Satisfaction Score (CSAT), as well as qualitative feedback from interviews, focus groups, or social media posts.

Tip: *Promote a culture of continuous improvement* by discussing customer satisfaction metrics in team meetings and setting goals based on this feedback. Instilling a customer-centric culture across your organization is crucial to achieve truly successful products.

4. Embrace failure as an opportunity for growth.

As a product manager, you will inevitably face setbacks and failures. These moments, though difficult, can provide valuable opportunities to learn and grow as a professional. A customer-centric mindset encourages viewing mistakes as catalysts for change and focusing on using them to improve the product.

Tip: *Adopt a support network* by connecting with other professionals in the product management community. Share your experiences, insights, and challenges to benefit from collective wisdom and foster a more customer-centric approach in your field.

Deep insights:

1. Customer-centricity is not just about satisfying your customers; it's about exceeding their expectations. By going above and beyond in addressing their needs, you create a sense of loyalty and trust. This often translates into repeat business and positive word-of-mouth marketing that can strengthen your brand's standing in the long run.

2. The customer-centric mindset goes beyond the confines of product management. By developing strong partnerships with other departments, such as customer support, sales, and marketing, you can take

a holistic approach to customer success. This collaboration enables your organization to provide exceptional customer experiences, leading to increased trust and loyalty in your brand.

In conclusion, developing a customer-centric mindset is pivotal in the ever-evolving world of product management. By truly understanding and empathizing with your target audience, centralizing decision-making around their needs, focusing on customer satisfaction metrics, and learning from failure, you can become a stronger product manager and contribute significantly to your company's success.

Chapter 2: Experimentation and Hypothesis-Driven Development

one of the most effective approaches I've encountered is the emphasis on experimentation and hypothesis-driven development. This is a process that allows product managers to uncover truths and validate assumptions, ultimately resulting in the creation of better products. In this chapter, we'll dive into the what, why, and how of experimentation and hypothesis-driven development, and provide practical advice to help product managers take their craft to the next level.

2.1 Why should product managers care about Experimentation and Hypothesis-Driven Development?

As a product manager, it's easy to become attached to our ideas and vision. After all, we're the ones responsible for guiding the product development team to create a solution that addresses the needs of our customers. This can often lead to a narrow focus, where we assume we know what's best and disregard ideas or opinions that go against our beliefs.

But the truth is that product development is an ever-evolving process. Markets change, customers evolve, and competitors appear. To keep up and remain ahead, we need to adopt a mindset of continuous learning (Andriole, 2015). Experimentation and hypothesis-driven development provide the tool we need to validate our ideas and assumptions quickly and inexpensively.

Understanding the scientific method and experimentation

To successfully apply experimentation and hypothesis-driven development, we must first become well-versed in the scientific method. In essence, the scientific method is a series of steps intended to test theories through observation and experimentation (Norman & Draper, n.d.).

The scientific method can be broken down into five key steps:

1. Ask a question.
2. Conduct background research.
3. Formulate a hypothesis.
4. Design and run an experiment to test the hypothesis.
5. Analyze data and draw conclusions.

As product managers, our experiments serve as the bridge between our assumptions and the data that either supports or refutes them. By constantly refining and iterating based on the outcomes, we build better products in less time and with less cost.

Hypothesis-Driven Development: A framework for experimentation

Hypothesis-Driven Development (HDD) is a framework that incorporates the principles of the scientific method into product management. This consists of systematically constructing and testing hypotheses with the goal of validating or disproving assumptions about a product.

Here's a practical model to help you structure your HDD efforts:

1. Define the problem: Clearly identify the issue you're trying to solve or the opportunity you're seeking to address.

2. Formulate a hypothesis: Outline your proposed solution or approach based on your current understanding of the problem.

3. Determine key metrics: Identify the metrics that will indicate if your hypothesis is valid.

4. Design and run experiments: Create and execute an experiment plan that tests your hypothesis, ensuring that variables are carefully controlled.

5. Measure and analyze data: Record and evaluate the data to determine success or failure in meeting the desired outcomes.

6. Rinse and repeat: Use the insights gained to devise new hypotheses, design additional experiments, or adapt your approach.

Hands-on experimentation: Practical tips for product managers

Now that we understand the benefits and underlying principles of experimentation and hypothesis-driven development, let's explore some practical advice to help you make the most of this approach:

1. Start small and scale

Focus on small, incremental experiments to build up your confidence and encourage buy-in from your team. Simple A/B testing on a single feature or page could provide valuable insights that inform larger decisions about the overall product.

2. Collaborate

Involve your team in the hypothesis and experiment design process. By bringing together different perspectives and expertise, you're more likely to develop a valid hypothesis and design effective experiments (Teresa & Simon, 2012).

3. Stay objective

Focus on the data, not your own biases or opinions. Be open to the possibility that your hypothesis may be disproven and learn from those failures. As Reid Hoffman, founder of LinkedIn, famously said, "If you're not embarrassed by the first version of your product, you've launched too late."

4. Document the process

Keep detailed records of your hypotheses, experiments, and results. These records serve as invaluable information sources for future product development or experiments.

5. Adapt and iterate

Don't be afraid to pivot or iterate your product in response to your experiment findings. Embrace the insights and use them to strengthen your product.

Conclusion

Experimentation and hypothesis-driven development are essential tactics in the product manager's toolkit. They enable continuous learning, allowing us to create stronger products and grow as professionals. By mastering these practices, you'll set yourself and your team up for long-term success in the fast-paced world of product management.

2.2 A/B Testing

As we continue our journey to become stronger product managers, let's take a moment to discuss the importance of data and how it can help us make better decisions. One of the most powerful tools we have in our arsenal is A/B testing, a technique widely used in product management, marketing, and software development to determine the effectiveness of a given approach.

A/B testing, also known as split testing or bucket testing, is a method by which two or more versions of a product, webpage, marketing email, or any other user-facing element are served to different subsets of your user group. By gathering data and comparing the performance of each variant against a defined target metric or success criterion, you as a product manager can make evidence-based decisions to optimize your product or marketing strategy (Kohavi et al., 2009).

Before we delve into the details of setting up and executing an A/B test, it's essential to recognize the value of empathy and intuition in your role as a product manager. While data-driven decisions are critical, it's equally important to appreciate the nuances of human behavior and truly understand what drives your users. This harmonious blend of quantitative analysis and qualitative insight will enable you to make more strategic decisions on behalf of your users (Spool, 2007).

Now that we have an understanding of the importance of marrying data and empathy, let's dive into how to set up, run, and analyze an A/B test to derive deep insights that will help you make better, data-driven decisions.

Step 1: Identify your objective

As with any experiment, the first step in A/B testing is to determine your objective. As a product manager, your main goal may be to increase engagement, drive revenue, or improve overall user satisfaction. Knowing your goal will help you define clear and actionable hypotheses that can be tested through A/B tests, enabling you to gather meaningful insights from the results (Kohavi & Thomason, 2017).

A practical example to consider might be testing the effectiveness of two different calls to action, such as "Sign up now" vs. "Learn more," on your product's landing page. Your objective in this example might be to increase the number of sign-ups, and the variants being tested are the two different call-to-action buttons.

Step 2: Design your experiment

Designing an A/B test requires you to formulate a hypothesis and determine the appropriate sample size for each variation to ensure statistical significance. The hypothesis typically states that one variation is expected to be better than the other.

In our practical example, the hypothesis could be: "The new call-to-action button, 'Learn more,' will result in a higher sign-up conversion rate than the current button, 'Sign up now.'" The sample size you select for your test should be large enough to draw a meaningful conclusion, considering factors such as your expected effect size, desired significance level, and statistical power (Imbens & Rubin, 2015).

Step 3: Execute the test

Once you have designed your A/B test, it's time to implement the changes in the product, webpage, or email, and randomly assign users to different variations. It is essential to randomly assign users to avoid any potential bias in the results (Kohavi et al., 2009). You could use tools like Optimizely, VWO, or Google Optimize that provide a straightforward interface to create and execute A/B tests for different marketing channels and platforms.

Monitoring the performance of each variant during the test is crucial to ensure everything is working as intended and to make any necessary adjustments.

Step 4: Analyze the results

After the A/B test has concluded, it's time to analyze the results and determine if the hypothesis was supported by the data. This process usually involves comparing the performance of each variant concerning the key metric(s), in our case, the conversion rate, and determining if there's a statistically significant difference between the variants (Kohavi & Thomason, 2017).

If the results are statistically significant, it's time to draw conclusions from the test and implement the winning variant to improve the product or user experience based on the insights gained.

Conclusion

A/B testing is a powerful tool that, when used correctly, can help product managers collect actionable insights to optimize their products based on actual user data. By understanding and embracing this technique, you can effectively drive decisions that will have a tangible impact on your product's success.

Keep in mind, though, that A/B testing is just one of the many tools in a product manager's toolkit. Maintaining a balance between data-driven decisions and human-centered insights is crucial for your growth as a product management expert.

Deep insights to consider when using A/B testing:

1. How A/B tests can impact long-term user satisfaction versus short-term gains: Consider how changes made based on A/B test results might affect the long-term satisfaction of users, as opposed to only focusing on immediate performance improvements (Spool, 2007).

2. Limitations and potential pitfalls in A/B testing: It's essential to understand the limitations of A/B testing, such as localized learning, the potential for bias, and the possibility of over-optimization, leading to a suboptimal overall user experience (Kohavi & Thomason, 2017).

2.2 Multivariate Testing

As a product manager, you have probably heard of A/B testing – the process of comparing two versions of a webpage, app, or feature to see which one performs better. While A/B testing is an essential tool in your arsenal, you may still be missing out on a more comprehensive and powerful testing method: multivariate testing (MVT).

Multivariate testing allows you to test multiple variables simultaneously, helping you gain valuable insights into which combination of elements and features lead to the best outcomes. It is like conducting a series of A/B tests, but on a larger scale and in a more efficient manner. In this section, we will explore the benefits of MVT, best practices for implementing it, and how to interpret the results to make data-driven decisions for your product.

Why Multivariate Testing?

One of the primary advantages of MVT is that it allows you to test a wide range of permutations and combinations of elements on your product. This increases the likelihood of uncovering a winning combination that outperforms all other variants. A study by Sesame Communications (Wilson, 2013) demonstrates the power of MVT, where multivariate tests on dental practice websites led to a 69% increase in appointment bookings. By changing various elements such as header layouts, buttons, and colors, they were able to identify the most successful combination that attracted users.

The insights you gain from MVT are not just limited to a single webpage or feature but can be applied across your entire product. As product managers, having these insights at your disposal will help you make informed decisions and drive continuous improvement throughout your product's lifecycle.

Best Practices for Conducting Multivariate Tests

1. Define a clear objective: Before starting the testing process, identify which part of the customer journey or conversion funnel you want to optimize. It could be improving user engagement, increasing sign-ups or subscription rates, or boosting purchase completion, for example (Karr, 2019). Once you have a clear objective in mind, it will be easier to select the appropriate elements for testing and use the results more effectively.

2. Choose the right elements to test: It might be tempting to test every possible element on your page or feature; however, this approach can be counterproductive. As the number of tested elements increases, the complexity of the experiment and the required sample size also grow, potentially delaying the test's completion. Select the most crucial elements that are likely to have a significant impact on your objective and prioritize their testing.

3. Segment your audience: Keep in mind that different users might have different preferences or react differently to changes in your product. Segment your audience according to various criteria, such as demographics, device, or traffic source, to gain deeper insights into your users and ensure the results can be generalized effectively.

4. Don't stop at just one test: Just like A/B testing, MVT is an ongoing process. Just because you found a winning combination in the first experiment doesn't

mean it will always remain the best option. Regularly conduct new tests to adapt to changing user preferences and stay ahead of the competition.

Interpreting the Results

MVT results can be more challenging to interpret compared to A/B testing due to the larger number of tested combinations. But fear not, here are some tips to make sense of the results:

1. Focus on the most significant results: Draw attention to the combinations that have either outperformed or underperformed significantly compared to your current design or baseline. This will help you identify the high-impact changes you can make immediately to improve your product's performance.

2. Look for trends: Analyze the results for any patterns or trends that emerge across different variants. For example, you might notice that a certain color consistently performs well, regardless of other elements. By isolating trends, you can make informed design choices even beyond the scope of the specific test (Karr, 2019).

3. Calculate the confidence level: Just like A/B testing, make sure the results of your MVT are statistically significant. A higher confidence level means a lower risk of making incorrect decisions based on your test results. Aim for a confidence level of at least 95% to ensure the reliability of your findings.

Multivariate testing is a powerful technique that can unlock new levels of optimization and performance for your product. By carefully selecting the elements to test, conducting the experiments properly, and interpreting the results effectively, you can derive deep insights that will make you a stronger product manager.

As a closing thought, remember that the end goal of any testing method is not just to determine the winning combination of elements, but to drive continuous improvement and growth. Understanding your users and making data-driven decisions will help shape your product to meet their needs and expectations, solidifying your product's success in the long run.

2.3 User Testing and Feedback

As a product manager, you have the responsibility to build and refine your product to ultimately delight your customers. But how can you ensure that your product is actually effective in addressing their needs and solving their problems? One indispensable process you must incorporate into your product management strategy is user testing and feedback. In this section, we'll delve into the importance of user testing and feedback, various methods to carry out this process, and how to effectively analyze the data obtained to make more informed decisions.

User testing, also known as usability testing, is the process of evaluating your product by testing it with representative users, to identify any potential issues and gather insights, into the overall user experience. It is a critical part of building a strong product since it helps to validate your assumptions or discover new insights that directly come from the people who matter most - your customers (Nielsen, 1993).

One of the main benefits of user testing and feedback is to identify issues that you, as a product manager, may not have accounted for during the planning and design phase. Even the most sophisticated and experienced designers can fall into the trap of assuming that the product is perfectly designed for the target users (Dumas & Redish, 1999). This can lead to missed opportunities to address crucial pain points that may only be revealed through user testing.

Before we discuss how to effectively incorporate user testing into your product management strategy, it's important to understand some of the various methods and approaches available to you. Some of the most popular methods include:

1. Lab-based usability testing: In this method, users are observed while they interact with the product in a controlled environment, typically supervised by a moderator.

2. Remote usability testing: Users test your product remotely, often through online tests and surveys, and provide feedback by recording their experience or completing questionnaires.

3. Iterative prototype testing: Users are engaged throughout the development process, with multiple sessions for testing takes place during the different stages of your product's evolution.

4. A/B testing: Two different versions of a specific feature or a webpage, for example, are subjected to testing with users to identify which one is more effective in terms of user experience and key metrics.

While each method has its own benefits and limitations, the ultimate goal remains the same: to collect relevant data that will inform your product decisions, so that you can deliver delightful user experiences.

A core aspect of an effective user testing process is planning. You need to clearly outline the purpose of the test, define the tasks that the users will complete, and determine the data you wish to collect. Keep in mind that a major goal of user testing is to gather not only quantitative data about your product performance (such as conversion rates or time spent on a task) but also qualitative data on the user's feelings, preferences, and personal experiences.

One valuable insight shared by experts in the field is that user testing should not be a one-time, afterthought activity

(Nielsen, 2000). Instead, it should be an ongoing, iterative process that takes place throughout the product lifecycle. Keeping a constant feedback loop with your users can save you time and resources by spotting issues earlier in the development process, rather than trying to change an already-developed and feature-filled product.

Now, it's time to talk about how to effectively analyze the data obtained from user testing. First, it's crucial to differentiate between "noise" and "signal." Noise represents irrelevant or inconsequential information, while signals are meaningful and valuable insights that can guide your decision-making. Identifying these signals may require digging deeper into the feedback, asking follow-up questions, or conducting further tests to validate trends.

Moreover, it's essential to be open to negative feedback and not take it personally. Keep in mind that users are providing this feedback with the goal of improving the product. By embracing and acting upon criticism with humility, you're well on the way to creating a better product that provides a delightful user experience.

To wrap up, user testing and feedback are the backbone of creating user-centric products. As a product manager, it's not only your responsibility but also your greatest opportunity to leverage invaluable data and insights from your users. With a structured, iterative approach and a mindset open to constructive criticism, you'll become a stronger product manager, ultimately delivering products that truly serve and delight your customers.

Chapter 3: Data-Driven Decision-Making

As a product manager, making data-driven decisions is an essential part of your job. It's important not only because it allows you to solve management challenges more efficiently and objectively, but also because it helps you build a culture of problem-solving and continuous learning within your team. So, what exactly is data-driven decision-making, and how can you apply it to your role as a product manager? In this section, we'll explore the concept, as well as some practical advice that you can use to become a stronger product manager.

What is Data-Driven Decision-Making?

Data-driven decision-making is the process of making decisions by using data and analytics to support and inform them. It involves a systematic approach to gathering, analyzing, and interpreting data to make informed decisions based on facts rather than gut feelings, intuition, or assumptions. According to IBM (2021), data-driven companies are 19 times more likely to be profitable than those that don't utilize data effectively.

For product managers, making data-driven decisions can range from deciding the best product features to introduce or optimize, determining pricing for existing products, or identifying customer pain points that need addressing. The data used to make these decisions might include user behavior, customer feedback, or industry trends, among other types of data.

The Importance of Data-Driven Decision-Making

Why is data-driven decision-making so essential for product managers? Here are some of the key benefits:

1. Improved decision quality: By using data to inform your decisions, you increase the likelihood that they'll

be successful. Data can help you identify the most pressing problems, derive insights about customer behavior, and uncover new opportunities.

2. Efficiency: It takes less time to make decisions based on data than it does to rely on gut feelings or intuition. Data-driven decision-making also enables you to monitor the effectiveness of your decisions, allowing for adjustments as needed.

3. Reduced bias: Relying on data helps to eliminate biases in decision-making, as it allows you to approach problems more objectively.

4. Greater adaptability: Data-driven decision-making allows you to adapt quickly to changing market conditions or competitor activity, enabling you to respond effectively and maintain a competitive edge.

How to Apply Data-Driven Decision-Making as a Product Manager

Now that we've established the importance of data-driven decision-making, let's look at some practical steps you can take to implement it in your day-to-day role as a product manager.

1. Embrace a data-driven mindset: This starts with setting an expectation within your team that data will be used to guide decision-making. Encourage collaboration between stakeholders and ensure they understand the value of a data-driven approach.

2. Identify key metrics: To make data-driven decisions, it's important to first identify the metrics most relevant to your products and business goals. Having a clear understanding of these metrics will enable you to more effectively measure the impact of your decisions.

3. Collect the data: Ensure that your team has access to the data you need to make informed decisions. This might include data from analytics tools, customer surveys, or third-party sources such as market research.

4. Analyze the data: Once you have the data, take the time to properly analyze it. This might involve creating dashboards to visualize trends or using advanced analytics techniques such as predictive modeling to make more accurate predictions about potential business outcomes.

5. Communicate results: A critical part of data-driven decision-making is being transparent about the results of your analyses. Share your findings with your team and stakeholders, and use the insights you've gained to inform discussions about strategic planning and product development.

When it comes to implementing these practices, it's crucial not to forget the human element in the decision-making process. Research conducted by Kellog Insight (2019) emphasizes that while data is essential, too much reliance on data can be detrimental, especially in complex situations where human judgment is more accurate. With this in mind, strive to find the balance between utilizing data effectively and leveraging your experience and judgment.

Deep Insights

To wrap up this section, let's explore two deep insights that can help you make better data-driven decisions as a product manager.

1. Adopt a hypothesis-driven approach: Before making decisions or implementing new features, form a hypothesis about the expected outcome. This approach allows you to test the validity of your assumptions against the available data and refine

them as needed. You can then make more informed decisions based on the outcomes of your hypotheses.

2. Understand the limitations of your data: Recognize that data is not always perfect and can sometimes be limited or even misleading. For instance, a small sample size can lead to biased results, or data might not be representative of your target audience. Always consider potential biases and limitations in your data when making decisions.

In conclusion, adopting a data-driven decision-making approach as a product manager can improve the quality of your decisions, reduce biases, and increase efficiency. By embracing a data-driven mindset, identifying key metrics, collecting and analyzing data, and finding the balance between data and human judgement, you'll be on your way to becoming a stronger product manager.

3.1 Metrics and key performance indicators (KPIs)

As a product manager, one of your essential tasks is to measure the success and health of your product. Metrics and key performance indicators (KPIs) are the tools that help you quantitatively understand and visualize your product's performance. In this section, we will explore the importance of metrics, the various types of KPIs, challenges in selecting the right metrics, and some practical advice on utilizing them effectively.

Firstly, why are metrics and KPIs critical? Accurate measurement helps you identify problems and opportunities, set goals, and track progress towards those goals (Eisenmann, 2020). By gathering relevant data and analyzing it thoroughly, you can make informed decisions and optimize your product strategy. Moreover, when you share these insights with your team and stakeholders, it promotes clear communication and drives alignment.

There are several types of metrics that cater to specific product management aspects. Commonly, they can be categorized into four types: usage, engagement, satisfaction, and financial (Gupta, 2016). Usage metrics focus on how often your customers use your product and the features they use most. Examples include monthly active users, daily active users, and product adoption rates. Engagement metrics measure the depth and quality of your users' interactions with your product. Time spent on a platform, click-through rates, and net promoter scores (NPS) are some popular engagement KPIs. Satisfaction metrics offer insights into customer delight, reflecting the value your product provides. Customer satisfaction (CSAT) scores and churn rates are typical in this category. Lastly, financial metrics illustrate the monetary impact of your product. Examples include revenue, margin, and customer lifetime value.

Selecting the right KPIs is a challenging task for product managers (Kleiner, 2020). Keep in mind that too many metrics can lead to data overload and cloud your decision-making process. Before choosing a metric, examine whether it is:
a) Relevant to your product goals and strategy,
b) Easy to understand and communicate,
c) Measurable and reliable,
d) Actionable and influential.

Now that you have a solid understanding of metrics and KPIs, let's dive into some practical advice and deep insights for product managers:

1. **Look beyond vanity metrics:** Vanity metrics, such as total downloads or sign-ups, may look impressive but usually do not provide actionable insights. Instead, focus on metrics aligned with your core product objectives and customer needs. For example, if your product goal is to increase customer engagement, prioritize metrics like daily active users

or session lengths over more superficial ones like total app installs.

2. **Benchmark against competitors:** Understanding your product's performance in the context of the market is essential. Research competitor products and their KPIs to identify the industry standard and opportunities for differentiation. Align your team's aspirations with realistic expectations and celebrate what sets your product apart.

3. **Embrace iteratively refining KPIs:** As your product and market evolve, metrics that once seemed relevant might become obsolete or inadequate. Be open to updating or replacing KPIs as necessary to maintain their relevance and usefulness.

4. **Balance quantitative and qualitative data:** While metrics provide quantitative insights, qualitative data—such as customer feedback, interviews, and usability tests—complements your understanding of user behavior and preferences. Combining both types of data allows for a more comprehensive and accurate analysis of your product's performance.

Deep Insight 1: Metrics can trigger unintended consequences. An overemphasis on particular metrics may lead to team members manipulating data or engaging in behaviors that are not genuinely beneficial. For instance, let's say your team is laser-focused on increasing sign-up numbers above all else. This pressure can inadvertently result in low-quality sign-ups, which don't convert into engaged, paying customers (Eisenmann, 2020). Ensure that the KPIs you choose align with long-term goals and encourage the right behaviors within your team.

Deep Insight 2: Metrics can inform your product roadmap. Engaging your team in the metric-selection process can lead to collaboration and the identification of key initiatives that address product weaknesses or capitalize on strengths.

Integrate KPI tracking into your product planning cycle and encourage data-driven decision-making.

In conclusion, understanding and selecting the right metrics and KPIs are vital for product managers. From measuring product performance to driving alignment, metrics pave the path for informed decision-making, learning, and growth. By continually reassessing which metrics matter most and digging deeper into the real impact of your product, you and your team will undoubtedly become stronger product managers.

3.2 Analytics and Data Visualization

As a product manager, one of your core responsibilities is to make well-informed decisions that drive the success of the product you're managing. To make smart decisions, it is essential to leverage data and analytics, and effectively interpret the insights gleaned from these analyses.

An increasingly popular way to represent complex data is through data visualization – the use of graphical elements to showcase relationships, trends, and patterns in the information. This visual medium allows for a more accessible, easily digestible format that aids in understanding the data's implications clearly and quickly (Few, 2009). In this section, we'll explore the value of data visualization in product management and share some practical advice on how to integrate it into your workflow.

Why data visualization?

Before diving into the practical aspects, let's discuss why data visualization is vital in product management. First and foremost, it helps convey the story behind your data more effectively than raw numbers or text alone (Heer & Shneiderman, 2012). A well-designed visualization not only enhances the understanding of the underlying data but can also uncover hidden insights and relationships that might be overlooked in a traditional spreadsheet or report.

Data visualization offers several other benefits, including:

1. Simplified decision-making: Visual representations help you quickly grasp the most critical information, enabling you to make faster, more informed decisions.

2. Enhanced communication: It's often easier to communicate your findings and recommendations to stakeholders using visual aids rather than just sharing a set of numbers.

3. Improved collaboration: By making data readily accessible and intuitive, data visualization aids in fostering a shared understanding among team members, promoting collaboration.

Deep Insight #1: Visualization is not a one-size-fits-all solution. The same data can be represented in several ways, and the choice of visual representation depends on the context, objective, and audience. Be thoughtful in your approach to pick the visualization that best fits your needs and communicates your message effectively (Cairo, 2016).

Practical advice:

1. Understand your data: To create a meaningful visualization, you must start by familiarizing yourself with the data you're working with. Understand the relationships between variables, identify patterns and anomalies, and determine the critical insights you want to convey.

2. Define your objectives: Before you jump into creating visualizations, it's essential to have a clear understanding of what you're trying to achieve. Whether you want to explain a particular trend, showcase the performance of a feature, or highlight a problem, establishing your objective upfront will

ensure that your visualizations are purposeful and relevant.

3. Know your audience: A crucial aspect of creating effective visualizations is understanding your audience's preferences and aptitude for interpreting data. Tailor your visualizations according to their needs to ensure the intended message is effectively conveyed.

4. Use the appropriate tools: Several tools can help you create stunning visualizations with ease, ranging from simple ones like Excel and Google Charts to more advanced platforms like Tableau and D3.js. Choose a tool that best fits your needs, skillset, and the complexity of the data you're working with.

Deep Insight #2: Data visualization is an iterative process. Don't be afraid to refine and revise your visualizations based on feedback from your target audience. It's also crucial to validate the data and ensure its accuracy before presenting your findings, as incorrect assumptions or faulty logic can lead to poor decision-making.

In conclusion, incorporating analytics and data visualization into your product management practice can greatly enhance your ability to make informed decisions and communicate effectively with stakeholders. Don't be intimidated by the prospect of working with data – start small, iterate, and refine your visualizations over time. Soon, you'll be well-equipped to confidently leverage analytics and data visualization in your role as a product manager.

3.3 Leveraging Artificial Intelligence and Machine Learning

As a product manager, your role constantly evolves as technology advances, and one of the most significant developments affecting product management in recent years is the rise of artificial intelligence (AI) and machine learning

(ML). These powerful tools have the potential to transform not only the products you create but also the methods you use to develop and manage them. In this section, we'll explore how you can leverage AI and ML to become a stronger product manager.

AI and ML can be powerful allies in your quest to develop better products faster. From providing insights through data analysis to improving business processes, AI and ML have the potential to make your job easier and more impactful. Let's dive deeper into how you can utilize AI and ML to your advantage in product management.

Understanding AI and ML capabilities

Before we discuss how to leverage AI and ML, it's important to understand their capabilities. AI is the broader term that refers to machines or computers mimicking human intelligence. ML, a subset of AI, is the process by which machines learn from data and make predictions or decisions without explicit programming.

As a product manager, you might come across AI-powered tools that can analyze vast amounts of data to identify patterns, trends, and correlations. For instance, AI-driven analytics tools can help you understand customer behavior, market trends, and competitive landscape. On the other hand, ML-powered applications can make predictions and generate recommendations, like determining optimal pricing or segmenting users based on their preferences.

Leveraging AI and ML for data-driven decision making

In today's data-driven world, successful product managers know how to leverage data to make informed decisions throughout the product life cycle. One key to success is to apply AI and ML tools to derive actionable insights from your data (Singh, 2020).

For instance, AI-powered analytics tools can identify friction points in user experience and churn risk indicators, enabling you to make data-driven decisions on product enhancements and customer retention. ML algorithms can analyze historical product usage data, churn rates, and customer feedback to understand patterns and further optimize the product experience.

Research by McKinsey shows that companies that leverage AI and ML for decision-making report significant improvements in business outcomes, including revenue growth and cost reduction (Bughin et al., 2017). As a product manager, embracing AI and ML can give you an edge in making decisions that have a positive impact on your product's performance.

Insight 1: Implementing AI and ML in product development processes

Incorporating AI and ML into your product development process can create a significant competitive advantage. Research suggests that companies integrating these technologies into new product development are more likely to achieve above-average financial performance (Niewöhner et al., 2019). To take advantage of AI and ML, consider the following practical advice:

1. Integrate AI and ML into your product vision: Instead of considering AI and ML as add-ons, think of them as core components of your product. This approach will help you identify opportunities where AI and ML can enhance product functionality, user experience, and differentiation, right from the ideation stage.

2. Understand the limitations of AI and ML: It's important to recognize that AI and ML do not always provide perfect results. Be realistic about what they can and cannot achieve, and be prepared to iterate and refine models as you incorporate feedback from users and gather more data.

3. Collaborate with your data science team: Working closely with data scientists and engineers can help you understand how to incorporate AI and ML effectively, while also helping them grasp the business context and overall product objectives.

Insight 2: Building ethical AI and ML products

As product managers, it's crucial to consider the ethical implications of AI and ML products. Discrimination, privacy violations, and job loss concerns are just a few examples of the issues that may arise when integrating AI and ML (Kaplan, 2019). By addressing these concerns, you not only create products that are more likely to be accepted by users and regulators, but you also contribute to a more ethical AI and ML-enabled future.

1. Be transparent: Help users understand how AI and ML are used within your product and how their data will be processed.

2. Prioritize data privacy and security: Work closely with data scientists and engineers to ensure that user data is securely stored and accessed only by authorized parties.

3. Design products that are inclusive and unbiased: Make sure your data sets are diverse to avoid perpetuating biases, and carefully evaluate the ethical implications of your product's recommendations or predictions.

In summary, leveraging AI and ML can provide a significant boost to product managers who want to create more impactful products and make data-driven decisions that drive business success. By understanding AI and ML capabilities, integrating these technologies into your product development process, and adopting ethical practices, you'll be well on your way to becoming a stronger product manager.

Chapter 4: Mastering Product-Market Fit

I know that the holy grail of successful product management is achieving product-market fit. In this section of the book, we will explore the concept of product-market fit, learn how to measure it, and discuss best practices for aligning your product with your target market.

Definition of Product-Market Fit

Product-market fit is defined as the degree to which a product satisfies a strong market demand. In simpler terms, it means that you have built a product that customers want and are willing to pay for (Marc Andreessen, 2007). When your product meets the needs of your target audience and addresses their pain points, you're on your way to winning the game.

Achieving product-market fit is essential because it is the foundation of a sustainable business. Companies that fail to achieve this fit are more likely to struggle with sales, customer retention, and profitability (Lee et al., 2020).

Measuring Product-Market Fit

To measure product-market fit, it's important to focus on customer satisfaction and engagement. One useful metric to gauge customer satisfaction is the Net Promoter Score (NPS). NPS asks customers whether they would recommend the product to others, and the resulting score can give you an overall understanding of how much customers value your product (Reichheld, 2003).

Another effective way to measure product-market fit is by monitoring the insights and feedback that your customers provide. This can be done through customer interviews, surveys, and monitoring user engagement on your platform.

By keeping a pulse on how your users are interacting with your product and what aspects they find most valuable, you can better understand if your product is meeting their needs.

Deep Insights

1. Different Stages of Product-Market Fit

An important insight is that product-market fit is not a one-time event but is experienced in stages. Rahul Vohra, the founder of Superhuman, has identified three levels of product-market fit: Problem-Solution Fit, Product-Experience Fit, and Business-Model Fit (Vohra, 2018).

Problem-Solution Fit: At this stage, you have found a problem that enough customers are struggling with and have a potential solution. This phase involves validation through customer interviews, testing your market assumptions, and refining your value proposition.

Product-Experience Fit: This level is about creating an excellent product experience for customers. It requires delivering high-quality user experience, ensuring seamless interactions, and addressing all dimensions of a user's interaction with your product (contextual, emotional, technical).

Business-Model Fit: At this stage, the focus is on generating revenues through effective pricing, distribution, and promotion strategies. Business-model fit involves understanding the main cost drivers and the competitive landscape to ensure a viable, scalable, and profitable business.

2. Iterative Approach and Organizational Alignment

A key insight to achieving product-market fit is adopting an iterative approach throughout the product development process. The Lean Startup methodology popularized by Eric Ries encourages an iterative, customer-centric approach to product development (Ries, 2011). It's important to test your assumptions early and often, and to make rapid adjustments based on customer feedback.

Additionally, achieving product-market fit should not be solely the responsibility of the product management team. Success necessitates cross-functional collaboration and organizational alignment. From marketing to engineering, every team should focus on understanding the target customer and delivering value through tailored experiences.

Practical Advice

1. Clearly Define Your Target Market

To maximize your product's chances of achieving product-market fit, it's crucial to define your target market as specifically as possible. Create detailed customer profiles and personas that outline demographics, behaviors, preferences, and pain points.

2. Constantly Refine Your Value Proposition

As you gather customer feedback and insights, continuously refine your value proposition. This involves both iterating on your product as well as crafting compelling messaging that conveys the benefits of your product to your target audience.

3. Align Your Team around a Common Vision

Ensure that everyone on your team – from engineering to customer success – understands the target market and the problem your product aims to solve. This alignment will ensure smooth product development and effective launch and marketing efforts.

In conclusion, mastering product-market fit is a critical part of product management, which requires an ongoing focus on customer understanding, iteration, and organizational alignment. Keep these concepts in mind as you build and refine your products, and you'll be well on your way to becoming a stronger product manager.

4.1 Identifying Target Segments and Personas

Imagine you are playing darts, and you have the perfect aim, sharp focus, and a well-practiced technique. But what if you don't know where the dartboard is? You can't hit a target you don't see. In the realm of product management, knowing your target audience is akin to having a clear sight of the dartboard. You need to know who your customers are, what they want, and how your product can cater to their needs. This is where target segments and personas come into play. In this section, we'll dive deep into how to nail down these two critical components of product management.

First, let's understand the difference between segments and personas. A target segment refers to a specific group of customers, usually defined by demographics or other measurable attributes, while a persona is a semi-fictional representation of an ideal customer within that segment, encompassing their characteristics, goals, and challenges (Arnett, German & Hunt, 2003). Both concepts are essential, as identifying segments helps you to understand the market better, and personas allow you to empathize with your customers on a deeper level.

1. Identifying Target Segments

Start by listing the potential target segments for your product. Remember that not everyone in the market will be interested in what you have to offer, so think about who would find value in your product or service. While most traditional market segmentation methods focus on demographic, geographic, or psychographic factors, it's essential to consider the customer's needs and problems as the foundation for your segmentation efforts (Ulwick & Bettencourt, 2008).

A study by Ulwick and Bettencourt (2008) showed that "customer needs-based" segmentation yielded better results than "customer type-based" segmentation. In other words, instead of focusing solely on age or income levels, you should also take into account the specific problems your product can solve for each customer group. For example, if you're building a fitness app, one segment could be busy professionals who want to exercise but struggle to find the time, while another could be parents who want to stay in shape while juggling family responsibilities.

Once you have established the different segments, prioritize them based on several factors: potential for growth, profitability, accessibility, and alignment with your company's capabilities and vision. Spending time on this prioritization process will enable you to allocate your resources and focus your team's efforts effectively.

2. Developing Personas

After identifying and prioritizing your target segments, it's time to dig deeper into their motivations, desires, and pain points by creating personas. These fictional representations of your customers should be based on real-life data and insights gathered from interviews, surveys, and other forms of research.

A well-developed persona includes:

- Demographic information: Age, gender, education, profession, and location

- Behavioral characteristics: Online habits, hobbies, and preferences

- Goals and motivations: What they want to achieve and what drives them

- Pain points and challenges: The problems they face that your product can solve

- Brand interactions: How they engage with your brand and competitors

McDonald and Dunbar (2012) emphasized the importance of "deep understanding, empathy, and an affection for the customer" in designing products and marketing strategies. By fully grasping the customer's perspective, you can make informed decisions about product features, messaging, and user experience, leading to a more successful product.

One valuable insight shared by Herhold (2018) is that personas should not be limited to customers. In fact, creating internal personas can help you to address the challenges faced by various stakeholders within your organization, such as sales, engineering, or design teams. Developing an understanding of their perspectives can further streamline product development and collaboration.

In conclusion, the process of identifying target segments and building personas is not a one-time event. As markets change and your product evolves, it will be vital to revisit these personas, continuously learning from your customers, and adapting your strategy to remain relevant and competitive in the market. Remember, the key to a successful product is staying in tune with your customers' needs, and these target segments and personas are your guiding stars.

4.2 Crafting Compelling Value Propositions

I cannot stress enough the importance of crafting compelling value propositions for your products. A strong value proposition is the foundation of a successful product, as it clearly conveys the benefits your customers will gain from using your offering. This section will guide you on how to create value propositions that truly resonate with your target audience, ensuring your product stands out in the market.

But first, let's have a quick refresher on what a value proposition actually is. According to Michael Skok, creator of the Value Proposition Canvas, a value proposition is simply "an innovation, service, or feature intended to make a company or product attractive to customers" (Skok, 2013). In essence, it's the reason why customers will choose your product over others, by answering the question: "What problem does this product solve and/or what benefit will I gain from using it?"

To craft truly compelling value propositions, follow these essential tips:

1. Understand your customer's needs and desires.

A deep understanding of your target customers - their needs, desires, motivations, and pain points - is imperative for creating a value proposition that truly resonates with them. Conduct thorough market research, using both qualitative and quantitative methods, to gather this crucial customer data (Ulwick, 2005).

Practical advice: Run surveys, interviews, and focus groups to gain valuable insights directly from your target customers. Use online tools like Google Surveys, SurveyMonkey, or Typeform to run research surveys efficiently and cost-effectively.

2. Identify your product's unique selling points (USPs).

To stand out in the marketplace, you must understand what sets your product apart from the competition. This means identifying and articulating the unique selling points (USPs) of your product. USPs are the key differentiators that convince customers to choose your product over similar offerings (Kotler & Armstrong, 2010).

Practical advice: To identify your USPs, create a list of features and benefits that your product provides, consider your competitors' offerings, and then pinpoint the areas where your product excels. For example, if your product is an e-learning platform, are the pre-built assessments, engaging design, or the vast library of resources something that sets you apart from competitors?

3. Speak in benefits, not features.

While features are the characteristics of your product, benefits are the outcomes and improvements that customers can experience by using your product. Avoid focusing on the 'what' - the technical features of your product - and instead focus on the 'why' - the benefits your customers will enjoy. A strong value proposition emphasizes the positive change your product brings to your customers (Ulwick, 2005).

Practical advice: Instead of saying, "Our app has a predictive analytics feature," try something like, "Our app helps you make smarter decisions by predicting future outcomes based on historical data."

4. Keep it simple and specific.

An effective value proposition is concise, clear, and specific. It should be easily understood by your target customers and should avoid any ambiguity, jargon, or technical language that may confuse them.

Practical advice: Use simple language that your target audience can relate to, and keep your value proposition to one or two sentences, at most. Make sure it highlights the most important benefit of your product, and be as specific as possible. For example, "Our platform helps small businesses increase revenue by an average of 25% within the first six months of use."

Deep insights:

1. **Make it quantifiable:** Whenever possible, quantify the benefits of your product in concrete terms (e.g., "Save 10 hours per week," "Increase revenue by 25%"). This adds credibility to your value proposition and could deliver an extra persuasive punch.

2. **Test and refine:** Like any product-related communication, your value proposition will likely evolve as you learn more about your customers and

as your product matures. Don't be afraid to test different value propositions with your target audience, gather feedback, and refine your messaging as needed.

In conclusion, mastering the art of crafting compelling value propositions can significantly improve your product's chances of success. By understanding your customers, pinpointing your USPs, focusing on benefits, and using clear, concise, and specific language, you'll be well on your way to creating a value proposition that resonates with your target audience and sets your product apart from the competition.

4.3 Continuous Validation and Iteration

As a product manager, one of the keys to success is understanding that the process of building a great product never truly ends. It's not about reaching a specific milestone or delivering a feature-complete product; instead, you want to create a cycle of continuous validation and iteration to ensure that you're always providing the best possible value to users. Throughout this journey, you'll encounter new learnings, refine your hypothesis, and adjust your approach accordingly. Let's dive deeper into this critical aspect of product management.

In a highly dynamic and competing market, change is constant, and the only way to survive and thrive is to be adaptable (Sethi et al., 2020). As a product manager, you must face the reality that the moment you have "perfected" a product, someone else is already working on its better version. That's why it's crucial to always be validating your product ideas and iterating based on customer feedback and market trends.

An excellent example of continuous validation and iteration in action is Toyota's production process known as "kaizen" or continuous improvement. This approach promotes a culture of perpetual learning and improvement, through what is known as the **PDCA (Plan-Do-Check-Act) cycle**. Let's take a closer look at each step:

1. Plan: Establish the objectives and processes needed to deliver results in accordance with the expected outcomes.

2. Do: Implement the plan, execute the processes and collect data.

3. Check: Assess and analyze the actual results against the expected outcomes and identify any differences.

4. Act: Based on the analysis, take corrective actions and adjust the processes, as needed.

As you can see from the PDCA cycle, iteration is at the heart of the process. Being a product manager means being committed to continuous validation, learning, and iteration. So, how can you practically apply this to your day-to-day work? Here are some insights and advice.

Deep insight #1: Embrace the data-driven mindset

Instead of relying on your gut feelings or limited anecdotal evidence, make it a habit to collect actionable data that informs your decision-making process. Quantitative data is key for supporting or refuting assumptions, measuring the impact of your actions, and ultimately guiding product development in a more effective manner. Be it customer surveys, web analytics, or A/B experiments, invest in tools and techniques that help you gather the data required to validate your product ideas and inform your iterations.

Deep insight #2: Iterate fast and often

According to Eric Ries in his book, The Lean Startup, one of the core principles is to shorten the cycle between building and learning (Ries, 2011). By iterating quickly and frequently, you can identify flaws or shortcomings, learn from them, and make the necessary improvements sooner rather than later. Investing time and resources in building something only to find out that it doesn't meet users' needs can be a frustrating, costly mistake (Ries, 2011). Adopting agile methodologies, such as Scrum or Kanban, can help you incorporate iterations into your regular product development workflows.

Here are some more practical tips to foster continuous validation and iteration in your product management practice:

- Start with small, manageable experiments: Test your hypotheses on a small scale before committing to significant changes. This approach can help minimize the risk of failure and provide valuable insights to inform more significant initiatives.

- Leverage feedback from real users: User feedback is a goldmine of information that allows you to improve and optimize your product continuously. Schedule regular opportunities for users to interact with your product, either through beta testing, user interviews, or usability testing.

- Make learning a priority: Encourage your team to develop a learning culture that values curiosity, continuous improvement, and embraces failure as a learning opportunity. By instilling this mindset, your team will be more inclined to collaborate on iterating and improving your product over time.

- Be open to change: Staying flexible and adaptable to new information is critical to continuous validation and iteration. Embrace change as an opportunity to improve and evolve rather than resisting it because of sunk costs or pride.

Continuous validation and iteration are essential for successful product management. By staying committed to this mindset and consistently applying these techniques, you can make data-driven decisions, respond quickly to market changes, and ultimately create products that deliver maximum value to users.

Chapter 5: Advanced Tools and Methods for Product Managers

 I can't emphasize enough the importance of having the right tools and methods to become a stronger product manager. In an ever-evolving industry, it's crucial to stay up-to-date with advanced techniques that will help you achieve success, make more informed decisions, and ultimately, deliver better products. In the following section, I will present some valuable tools and methods, along with the practical advice and deep insights you need to tackle your ambitious goals.

Artificial Intelligence and Machine Learning

These days, it's hard to find a technology that's more impactful than Artificial Intelligence (AI) and Machine Learning (ML). According to a study conducted by Peltarion (2019), 83% of business leaders agree that AI and ML have the potential to change how their industries function. Product managers can utilize the power of AI and ML in various ways, such as improving the customer experience, automating repetitive tasks, or getting insights to make data-driven decisions.

One application area is using AI to analyze large amounts of customer feedback through sentiment analysis or natural language processing. By identifying patterns, product managers can find out what customers' pain points are and tailor the product roadmap accordingly.

For instance, platforms like MonkeyLearn can be integrated into your support tools to provide sentiment analysis on customer tickets or reviews. Similarly, Hugging Face API and OpenAI's GPT-3 can be utilized for text classification and summarization, based on machine learning.

Deep Insight: Integrating AI and ML into your product management tools can significantly improve the speed of the decision-making process, as these technologies can analyze vast amounts of data much faster than a human would. However, it's important to maintain oversight and not solely rely on AI, as there may still be some gaps in the analysis.

Research-driven Product Management

Research-driven product management emphasizes the significance of conducting research to guide product development. Doing research by collecting and analyzing customer data, market trends, and user behavior, allows product managers to make decisions based on evidence rather than intuition. A research by Markowitz et al. (2019) demonstrates how research-driven product management leads to more successful products.

One method for conducting research is through Design Thinking, a human-centered approach that focuses on understanding customers' needs and iterating solutions. Design Thinking consists of several stages such as empathizing, defining, ideating, prototyping, and testing. During these stages, product managers can conduct interviews, surveys, focus groups, and conduct usability studies to gather qualitative and quantitative data.

Another method is Lean Startup Methodology, which encourages experimenting, building a Minimum Viable Product (MVP), and quickly iterating based on customer feedback. By learning from each iteration, product managers can focus on building features that customers need and value, thereby reducing waste and accelerating product development.

Deep Insight: Integrating research-driven methodologies into your current product management practice can provide you with a more sound basis for developing products. Using these methodologies in conjunction with AI/ML tools can help validate findings, reduce bias, and create a more comprehensive picture of the market and user needs.

Advanced Analytics Tools & Visualization

Advanced analytics tools can significantly improve a product manager's decision-making process. By leveraging the power of data, product managers can gain insights into the performance of their products, inform the development process, and fine-tune strategies for greater success.

These tools include:

1. Amplitude and Mixpanel: These analytics tools provide insights into user behavior within your products. They track user actions, identify patterns, and provide a rich feature set for understanding customer journeys in apps and websites.

2. Tableau: A powerful data visualization tool, Tableau allows you to create interactive and shareable dashboards – ideal for visually presenting data at team meetings or to stakeholders.

3. Google Analytics: Track website usage and engagement metrics, with integrations to help identify key segments, understand user acquisition channels, and optimize your marketing efforts.

4. A/B Testing Tools: Tools like Optimizely and Google Optimize facilitate running experiments on product features and marketing campaigns to help you identify the best performing options.

Practical Advice: When using advanced analytics tools, it's crucial to establish clear Key Performance Indicators (KPIs) to monitor and measure product success. Keep a close eye on these KPIs and constantly reevaluate if they align with your product goals.

In conclusion, leveraging advanced tools and methods such as AI and ML, research-driven product management, and analytics tools can significantly improve a product manager's decision-making process and help them deliver success in their role. With this understanding, you can become a stronger product manager, capable of delivering outstanding products in a fast-paced, ever-changing world.

5.1 User Story Mapping and Journey Mapping

I have always underscored the importance of deeply understanding the user's perspective in order to create a successful product. A big part of that process involves mapping out user stories and user journey maps. So, strap in as we delve into these two essential tools for creating meaningful and effective products tailored to the end user.

While user story mapping and user journey mapping may sound similar, they serve different purposes in the product management process. However, both are related in that they provide crucial insights into user needs, behaviors, and motivations.

User Story Mapping

User story mapping (USM) is a visual representation of the user's experience with a product. It is a collaborative technique that involves working with your team to identify the vital aspects of the product and how they relate to the user's needs (Patton, 2014).

A study by Lucassen et al. (2016) highlights the benefits of USM in prioritizing and planning product development. The research found that user story mapping allowed teams to understand complex features and prioritize user needs more effectively.

To create a user story map, follow these steps:

1. Define the user persona: Start by creating a user persona, which represents your target audience. This

will help you keep focus on the end user's needs throughout the process.

2. List user activities: Identify the main tasks that a user typically performs when engaging with your product. To create the backbone of your user story map, write these main activities on cards or sticky notes, and place them horizontally in sequential order.

3. Break down activities into user stories: Under each main activity, write down the more specific tasks that a user performs, again in sequential order. These are your user stories.

4. Prioritize user stories: Arrange and prioritize the user stories vertically under each activity to reflect their importance.

5. Group stories into releases: Define product releases as groups of user stories that can be delivered incrementally. This sets the stage for agile development and continuous improvement.

User Journey Mapping

User journey mapping (UJM) is another powerful tool to design products that resonate with users. It focuses on the user's experience with the product over time, showing the full context of their interactions (Kalbach, 2016).

This comprehensive process allows product managers to visualize the entire user journey, uncover pain points, and identify opportunities for improvement. According to a case study by Stickdorn and Hormess (2016), UJM can lead to substantially increased customer satisfaction and improved business performance.

To create a user journey map, follow these steps:

1. Define the user persona: Similar to USM, start by creating a user persona to keep the focus on the end user.

2. Outline the stages: Identify the stages of the user's journey, from the initial interaction with your product to the final goal. Place these stages horizontally in your map.

3. Identify touchpoints: Determine the specific points of interaction between the user and your product during each stage.

4. Map the user's experience: For each touchpoint, detail the user's thoughts, emotions, and actions. This is where a comprehensive understanding of the user's needs, motivations, and frustrations will help you.

5. Identify opportunities: After analyzing the entire user journey, identify opportunities for improvement – whether it's addressing pain points or enhancing the overall experience.

Deep Insights

1. **Complementarity:** While USM and UJM serve different purposes, using them together can provide a richer understanding of your users. USM helps you break down product features based on user tasks, while UJM shows how users experience your product across different touchpoints. By combining these methods, you can develop a more user-centric product, leading to higher satisfaction and greater success.

2. **Collaboration:** Both USM and UJM are collaborative activities that involve cross-functional teams. Including perspectives from people with various skillsets (such as designers, developers, and business analysts) improves the overall

understanding of user needs and leads to better decision-making in the product development process.

In conclusion, user story mapping and user journey mapping are indispensable tools for understanding and addressing user needs. By integrating them with your product management process, you create a strong foundation for user-centered development that leads to successful products and satisfied customers.

5.2 Rapid Prototyping and MVP Development

Welcome back to our journey towards becoming a stronger product manager. In this section, we will discuss rapid prototyping and Minimum Viable Product (MVP) development, two essential methodologies that will surely enhance your product management skills. By understanding and using rapid prototyping and MVP development effectively, you can create better and more efficient products that meet the needs of your customers. So let's dive in!

Rapid Prototyping

Simply put, rapid prototyping is the process of quickly creating physical or functional models of a product to validate its design, performance, and usefulness. Product teams often use rapid prototyping to iterate between design, user feedback, and development to improve a product before it reaches the market (Houde & Hill, 1997).

Now, this might seem like an interesting and straightforward idea, but the real value comes when we delve deeper into its practical applications. Rapid prototyping has several benefits, including:

1. Reducing time and cost by quickly identifying potential issues and refining the design.

2. Improving communication within the team and with stakeholders by providing a tangible representation of the final product.

3. Enhancing decision making by presenting alternatives and enabling comparisons to choose the most appropriate design.

One key insight is not to confuse rapid prototyping with creating a perfect, polished product. Instead, the focus should be on using simple, quick, and cost-effective methods like sketching or virtual mockups to get feedback and minimize iteration cycles (Buchenau & Fulton Suri, 2000). This approach will allow you to learn and test ideas faster, ultimately leading to a better and more successful product.

MVP Development

MVP, or Minimum Viable Product, is a product version with just enough features to satisfy early adopters and collect valuable feedback for future development. The idea was popularized by Eric Ries in his book, "The Lean Startup." The MVP is a key concept to understand, as it directly ties to rapid prototyping by balancing time, cost, and value in product development (Ries, 2011).

The purpose of an MVP isn't to create a scaled-down version of your ultimate product vision. Instead, it's about validating your core value proposition and crucial assumptions about your market and users.

Here are some benefits you can get from building an MVP:

1. Reduced time to market: You can create and launch an MVP within a limited timeframe, allowing you to get to market faster and learn from real-world users.

2. Risk mitigation: By testing your core assumptions, you can identify and address potential risks early in the development process.

3. Resource optimization: Focusing only on the essential features maximizes the use of your resources and helps you control development costs.

Creating an MVP may seem like a straightforward process, but it's essential to recognize that your MVP should be more than just a simple version of the product. One deep insight is that you need to ensure that the MVP fulfills the needs of your target customers and provides value for them. Though the MVP may have fewer features, it should still be good enough to generate meaningful feedback and foster strong customer relationships (Maurya, 2012).

Practical Tips for Rapid Prototyping and MVP Development

To make the most of rapid prototyping and MVP development, consider the following advice:

1. Embrace a user-centered design approach: Start your process by understanding your users' problems and goals. Create personas and outline the user's journey to ensure that you're building something that they'll find valuable.

2. Iterate often: Don't wait until you have a perfect prototype or MVP; start by creating rough drafts and improving them based on feedback from users and stakeholders.

3. Learn to prioritize: Focus on the critical features and assumptions that need testing, but also be prepared to let go of features that may not deliver as much value. Remember, you can always integrate new features and improvements in future updates.

4. Be open to change: Based on feedback, be prepared to pivot, modify, or even scrap your initial idea if the results show that it isn't feasible or desirable.

5. Collaborate: Engage your team and stakeholders during the prototyping and MVP development processes. Build a culture of ongoing collaboration that nurtures trust, openness, and psychological safety.

In conclusion, rapid prototyping and MVP development are effective methodologies that can help you create better products by minimizing iteration cycles and focusing on validating core assumptions. By understanding and implementing these concepts, you'll be one step closer to becoming a stronger product manager.

Now that you're armed with these insights, it's time to get out there and start prototyping! In the next section, we'll cover the topic of user testing to ensure that your product not only meets your customers' needs but also delights them.

5.3 Jobs-to-be-done Framework

I cannot emphasize enough the importance of understanding your customers and their needs. A useful approach for achieving this understanding is the Jobs-to-be-done (JTBD) framework. As we delve into this section, let me share with you some valuable insights, research findings, and practical advice on how to use the JTBD framework to become a stronger product manager.

First, let's define the framework. The Jobs-to-be-done framework is a concept introduced by Clayton Christensen in his book "The Innovator's Solution" (Christensen, 2003). It posits that customers "hire" products and services to perform specific jobs in their lives. This idea is based on the assumption that people do not buy products or services for their features, but rather for what they can help them accomplish (Christensen et al., 2016).

As a product manager, understanding the JTBD framework can provide you with critical insights that can help you identify customer needs, design better products, and create targeted marketing strategies. By applying this framework, you essentially focus on customer goals and situations rather than trying to predict what features or functionalities they might want.

To demonstrate the JTBD framework's practicality, let's explore the two principal components: the functional job and the emotional job.

1. **Functional Job:** This refers to the main task or problem that customers want to resolve or achieve. In the context of the JTBD framework, it's essential to understand that customers don't really care about the product or service itself – they only care about the outcome it provides (Christensen et al., 2016).

For example, consider a customer who buys a power drill. They are not interested in the drill itself – what they truly want is a hole in the wall. As a product manager, your focus should be on identifying such functional jobs and creating products or services aimed at solving them.

2. **Emotional Job:** The emotional component of the JTBD framework concerns the feelings and experiences that customers associate with the resolution of their functional jobs. These emotional jobs can be both positive (i.e., satisfaction or pride) or negative (i.e., frustration or disappointment).

To create compelling products and services, you should aim to address both functional and emotional jobs. According to research by Bettencourt et al. (2014), addressing the emotional components associated with functional jobs can enhance customer loyalty and positively influence their purchasing decisions.

Now, let me share a few practical tips on how to apply the JTBD framework as a product manager:

1. **Identify and Define Customer Jobs:** Begin by conducting thorough research to determine the

functional and emotional jobs that customers want to accomplish. This could involve interviewing customers, analyzing existing data, conducting surveys, or observing user behavior. By understanding the unique jobs of your customers, you can cater to their needs more effectively.

2. **Prioritize Jobs**: Not all jobs are equally important to your customers. After identifying various jobs, prioritize them based on factors like customer relevance, market size, competition, and your unique capabilities. This prioritization will enable you to focus on developing products and features that address the most crucial and valuable customer jobs.

3. **Design Products and Services:** Armed with a clear understanding of your customers' jobs, you can now design products and services that provide innovative solutions to their functional and emotional needs. By designing products that better accomplish these jobs, you will gain a competitive advantage in the marketplace.

4. **Measure Success:** To validate your product and strategy, track metrics tied to the performance of your customers' jobs. By measuring success using job-related metrics, you can ensure that your products and features genuinely address customer needs and drive value for your organization.

Applying the JTBD framework doesn't stop once a product is launched; it's a continuous cycle. As customers discover new needs and competitors respond to your innovations, you must stay vigilant and adapt your approach accordingly.

In summary, the Jobs-to-be-done framework is a valuable tool for product managers to focus on customer needs and design products that genuinely add value to their lives. Integrating this approach into your product management practice will ultimately make you a stronger product manager and contribute to your organization's overall success. So, I encourage you to embrace this powerful framework and leverage it to unlock new opportunities and drive growth.

5.4 Kano Model for Prioritizing Features

one of the most critical aspects of the role is understanding how to prioritize features for your product. Deciding which features to include and which to leave out is one of the most challenging aspects of the job. One excellent tool for helping you make these difficult decisions is the Kano Model.

The Kano Model was introduced by Dr. Noriaki Kano in the 1980s as a means to prioritize product features based on customer satisfaction (Kano, 1984). It provides a unique lens through which to view customer preferences and has since become a valuable tool for product managers worldwide. In this section, we'll explore how the Kano Model works, discuss its strengths and weaknesses, and offer practical advice on how to use it effectively.

Understanding the Kano Model

At its core, the Kano Model groups product features into three categories (Tontini, 2017):

1. Must-be (M) - These are the features that customers assume will be present in a product. The absence of these features creates dissatisfaction among customers, but their presence does not necessarily lead to increased satisfaction. The must-be features are the basic requirements for customers to even consider the product.

2. Attractive (A) - These are the features that customers do not necessarily expect, but they would be delighted to find in a product. The presence of attractive features can significantly increase customer satisfaction, while their absence does not result in

dissatisfaction. Attractive features are the ones that can differentiate your product from the competition.

3. One-dimensional (O) - These features have a linear relationship with customer satisfaction – the more you add, the more satisfaction increases, up to a point of diminishing returns. These features are the ones that customers expect and actively look for when comparing products. While not as impactful as attractive features in differentiating your product, they still play a crucial role in influencing customer decisions.

It's worth noting that there may sometimes be a fourth category called "Indifferent," which refers to features that neither delight nor dissatisfy customers. These features don't have a significant impact on customer satisfaction, making them low-priority in most cases.

Practical Advice for Applying the Kano Model

Conduct customer research: Start by gathering feedback from your customers or potential customers. Surveys, interviews, and focus groups are all useful tools for understanding what features customers value, what they expect, and what would delight them. Remember to focus on a wide range of stakeholders, as the importance of different features may vary across different segments of the market.

Categorize and plot the features: Once you have collected sufficient feedback, categorize each feature according to the Kano Model. Then, plot the features on a graph with the x-axis representing investment needed and the y-axis representing potential customer satisfaction. This visualization helps to guide prioritization decisions by highlighting the features with the highest potential impact on customer satisfaction and market differentiation.

Cross-validate prioritization with other frameworks: While the Kano Model is helpful in prioritizing features, it's essential to cross-validate your decisions with other frameworks like the Value Proposition Canvas, Business Model Canvas, or Jobs-to-be-Done theory. Each of these frameworks offers different perspectives on the potential value and impact of features, ensuring a more comprehensive and holistic approach.

Deep Insights

Evolving customer perception of features: The Kano Model is not static – over time, features may shift categories as customer expectations evolve (Tontini, 2017). For instance, a feature that was once considered attractive could become a basic requirement as market norms change. This highlights the significance of continually conducting customer research to identify changes in perceptions and expectations, allowing you to adjust your feature prioritization accordingly.

Customizing the Kano Model for your industry: Different industries have unique dynamics that influence how customers perceive and value product features. For example, in industries with rapid technological advancements, some attractive features may quickly become must-be as competitors adopt them. In such cases, modifying the Kano Model to include more nuanced categorizations or adjusting the weight given to specific features within each category can help you better prioritize the features most valuable to your target customers.

In conclusion, the Kano Model is a powerful tool for guiding feature prioritization decisions. By understanding and categorizing features based on customer satisfaction, product managers can make more informed decisions about which features to prioritize. Continually conducting customer research, being aware of evolving customer perceptions, and customizing the Kano Model for your industry will help ensure your product continues to delight your customers and outshine the competition.

5.5 OKRs (Objectives and Key Results) for Goal-Setting and Alignment

you need to be able to establish clear and effective goals that align with the overall strategy of your organization. One powerful framework for achieving this is OKRs or Objectives and Key Results. Widely popularized by Google and other successful companies, OKRs can help you set ambitious goals and track progress, while also ensuring your team remains focused and accountable.

In this section, we will dive deep into the principles behind OKRs, discuss how they can benefit your product management efforts, and share some practical advice for implementing them within your organization. Along the way, we will highlight key findings from research papers and articles related to OKRs to further reinforce our points and provide you with actionable insights.

Understanding OKRs

At its core, OKRs consist of two crucial components: Objectives and Key Results. Objectives are the high-level goals you want to achieve, while Key Results are the specific, measurable outcomes that demonstrate progress towards your Objectives (Doerr, 2018). They provide teams with a way to set aspirational targets, improve focus and coordination, and foster a culture of learning and experimentation (de Mello, C., & da Silva, C. T., 2019).

One key insight from research on OKRs involves the importance of setting both incremental and stretch goals. A article published by Harvard Business Review (Latham, G. P., & Locke, E. A., 2006) found that when people are continually challenged with goals that are just beyond their current abilities, they experience increased motivation, better learning, and heightened feelings of accomplishment. Therefore, it's essential to find the right balance between easy-to-achieve targets and seemingly unreachable outcomes.

Another essential aspect of OKRs is the emphasis on aligning the team's goals with the company's overall objectives. This prevents siloed thinking and ensures everyone is working towards the same end-results. Research has shown that goal alignment is a critical factor in achieving high performance, as it enables employees to prioritize tasks, make better decisions, and collaborate more effectively (Kaplan, R. S., & Norton, D. P., 2001).

Practical Tips for Implementing OKRs

Now that we have a foundational understanding of OKRs let's discuss some practical strategies for implementing them within your organization:

1. Start small: If you're new to OKRs, consider starting with a pilot program for a specific team or project. This will allow you to test the waters, learn from your experiences, and refine your approach before rolling it out more broadly.

2. Set a limited number of Objectives and Key Results: Avoid overwhelming your team by limiting the number of OKRs they have to focus on at any given time. Aim for around 3-5 Objectives and 3-5 Key Results per Objective in order to maintain focus and drive accountability (Doerr, 2018).

3. Focus on measurable outcomes: Ensure that your Key Results are SMART (Specific, Measurable, Achievable, Relevant, and Time-bound). This will make it easier to track progress, assess performance, and make informed decisions as needed.

4. Establish a clear cadence for reviewing and updating OKRs: Regular check-ins are essential for maintaining alignment, fostering transparency, and promoting a continuous learning environment. Consider adopting a quarterly cycle to review and update your OKRs.

5. Encourage open communication and feedback: Cultivate a culture that values sharing progress updates, raising concerns, and providing feedback related to OKRs. This can help identify potential roadblocks or areas for improvement, as well as foster a sense of ownership and buy-in from team members.

Deep Insights for Maximizing OKR Success

To conclude this section on OKRs, let's discuss two critical insights that can help you maximize the effectiveness of this goal-setting framework within your product management efforts:

1. Embrace a culture of experimentation and learning: Adopting OKRs is an iterative process that requires a willingness to fail, learn, and adapt. Encourage your team to view setbacks as opportunities for growth and development. This growth mindset can help you extract valuable insights from both successful and unsuccessful initiatives, ultimately enabling you to make more informed decisions and drive better outcomes.

2. Balance agility with strategic alignment: OKRs are a powerful tool for fostering agility and responsiveness within your organization. However, it's crucial to ensure that this flexibility does not come at the expense of strategic alignment. Continuously reassess and realign your OKRs to ensure they remain in sync with your company's overarching objectives and changing market dynamics.

Ultimately, implementing and effectively utilizing OKRs can be a powerful catalyst for driving alignment, boosting motivation, and achieving better outcomes within your product management efforts. By embracing the principles and practices we've discussed in this section, you will be one step closer to becoming a stronger product manager.

it's my pleasure to share with you some advanced approaches you can utilize to level up your product management game. In this section, we will delve into the integration of new methodologies and cutting-edge techniques that will set you on a path to achieving outstanding results as a product manager.

Embracing an Agile mindset and optimizing cross-functional teams

If you haven't already, it's time to jump on the Agile bandwagon. "Agile" is more than a buzzword; it's a mindset that encourages flexibility, continuous improvement, and customer-centric development. According to research conducted by McKinsey & Company (2017), organizations that have embraced an agile mindset have reported significant gains in productivity and customer satisfaction.

To adopt an Agile mindset, it is imperative to form and lead cross-functional teams that consist of diverse skill sets, backgrounds, and perspectives. Encourage your team members to participate actively in all stages of the product lifecycle, including research, design, development, and testing. This promotes early and continuous feedback, resulting in a more robust end product.

Utilizing Data-driven decision-making

As a product manager, you need to make numerous decisions throughout the product's lifecycle. Leveraging data can help you make these decisions more effectively. Analyzing various data sources, including user interviews, customer reviews, and usage statistics, will enable you to spot trends and make informed decisions.

A study by MIT (Brynjolfsson, Hitt & Kim, 2011) shows that companies that make data-driven decisions observe 5-6%

higher productivity and profitability than those that don't. By grounding your decisions in concrete data, you not only enhance the credibility of your choices but also eliminate personal biases that may impact the final product.

Moreover, integrating data-driven insights accumulated through customer feedback, behavior analysis, and market research can help you identify gaps and potential improvements in your product, creating a better overall user experience.

Implementing the Lean Startup methodology

"The Lean Startup" by Eric Ries has become increasingly popular amongst product managers for its innovative approach to product development. At its core, the Lean Startup methodology aims to minimize waste and increase the likelihood of success by emphasizing speed, efficiency, and customer feedback.

The Lean Startup methodology entails creating a minimum viable product (MVP) — a predictive version of the product — and testing it in the market. By collecting data and feedback, product managers can determine what changes are needed before investing significant resources into full-scale development.

When you combine an Agile mindset, data-driven decision-making, and Lean Startup methodology, you create a powerful product management framework capable of quickly delivering innovative and valuable products to your customers.

Continuous learning and professional development

As a product manager, it is crucial to stay well-informed about emerging trends and tools in your domain. New methodologies and technologies can enhance your product management toolkit, while actively participating in workshops and conferences can sharpen your skill set and expand your knowledge base.

Continuous learning also involves staying in tune with your respective industry and staying informed about competitors, emerging startups, and advances in technology. Engaging in this information exchange will not only strengthen your product and marketing strategies but also enrich your professional network and open up new opportunities for collaboration.

Practice empathy and hone your storytelling abilities

Connecting with your customers and understanding their pain points is crucial in designing a product that effectively addresses their needs. As a product manager, practicing empathy allows you to envision, appreciate, and articulate the value proposition of your product, as well as facilitate meaningful and productive relationships with customers, stakeholders, and your team members.

Additionally, honing your storytelling ability is essential in shaping the narrative of your product. A compelling story can make your product stand out, resonate with your target audience, and persuade investors or stakeholders. By combining empathy with storytelling, you can create a deeply immersive experience, making it easier for others to recognize the value and potential of your product.

In conclusion, advanced approaches in product management go beyond just acquiring technical skills or certifications. They involve adopting new methodologies, utilizing data for decision-making, continuously learning, and enhancing your ability to empathize and tell compelling stories. By leveraging these techniques and refining your approach, you'll have a solid foundation to drive product success and thrive in your product management career.

6.1 Outcome-driven innovation

As product managers, we're always on the lookout for ways to create innovative products that satisfy customer needs and differentiate us from the competition. But what exactly is innovation, and how can we ensure we're heading in the right direction? I'd like to introduce you to the concept of outcome-driven innovation (ODI), an approach that's been proven to boost the success rate of new product development up to tenfold (Ulwick, 2002).

At its core, outcome-driven innovation is about understanding and prioritizing customer needs based on the outcomes they want to achieve. According to Anthony Ulwick, the pioneer of ODI, it shifts the focus from the features and functionality of products to the desired outcomes that customers want to achieve (Ulwick, 2002). Instead of chasing the latest technology trends or functionalities, ODI urges us to go deep into the hearts and minds of our customers to uncover the real value that would make their lives better. Let's discuss why this approach is so powerful and how you can apply it to your product management practice.

Deep insight #1: Putting customer outcomes first

One key aspect of outcome-driven innovation is changing the way we think about customer needs. Traditional approaches typically involve asking customers what features they want and then building the products accordingly. This often leads to uninspired, copycat offerings that struggle to differentiate themselves from the competition (Christensen et al., 2007).

ODI, on the other hand, puts customer outcomes at the center of the product development process. It posits that customers don't buy products for the sake of their features, but rather to get specific jobs done and achieve desired outcomes. In other words, people don't buy a drill because they want a drill; they buy it because they want to make holes in walls (Levitt, 1960).

"A job" in this context refers to a fundamental problem that customers are trying to solve, and the desired outcome is a measure of success when performing this job (Ulwick, 2005). By focusing on the outcomes that customers really care about, you're better able to create products that are both innovative and customer-centric.

Deep insight #2: Validating ideas through experimentation

ODI is not only about understanding what outcomes customers want to achieve, but also about validating the ideas by testing them in the market through experimentation. According to Eric Ries, author of "The Lean Startup," we should use a scientific approach to run experiments, learn from them, and iterate our products as fast as possible (Ries, 2011).

By validating our ideas through experiments, we can reduce the risk associated with developing a new product and ensure that we're pursuing the most innovative, outcome-driven solutions. This process may include techniques such as market research, interviews, prototyping, and testing to gather data on the effectiveness of our solutions and make data-driven decisions.

Practical advice for applying outcome-driven innovation

1. Identify the customer jobs to be done: Before you start building any new product or improving an existing one, you need to figure out the core jobs that your customers are trying to accomplish. You can use techniques like customer interviews, surveys, and observational research to determine these jobs.

2. Formulate desired customer outcomes: Once you've identified the jobs to be done, turn your attention to the outcomes customers want to achieve when

performing these jobs. You can uncover these outcomes through the same research methods mentioned earlier.

3. Prioritize customer outcomes: Don't assume that all customer outcomes are equally important. You need to prioritize them based on their importance to the customer, the relative underserved nature of the outcome, and the degree to which existing solutions are unsatisfactory.

4. Develop and refine product concepts: With a clear understanding of the desired customer outcomes, you can now start developing product concepts that deliver on these outcomes. Use prototyping, experimentation, and testing to iteratively refine your product concepts, ensuring they meet or exceed customer expectations.

5. Continuously track and measure progress: Once you've launched your product, continue to monitor its performance in the market and gather customer feedback. This will enable you to keep refining the product and ensure it stays aligned with customer needs and desired outcomes.

By embracing outcome-driven innovation, you can become a stronger product manager who consistently delivers innovative, customer-centric products. So, dig deep into your customers' minds and hearts, and create products that truly make their lives better. Remember, your ultimate goal is to enable your customers to achieve the desired outcomes and, in doing so, you will achieve lasting success in the market.

6.2: Systems Thinking for Product Design

As a product manager, you've probably experienced the frustration of releasing what you thought was the perfect product or feature, only to have it fail in the market or encounter unforeseen issues. Sometimes, these issues may even be the result of your "improvements." If this sounds familiar, you're not alone. It's common for people to feel blindsided when a system reacts differently, or even counter-intuitively, to well-meaning changes.

The issue is that, as humans, we tend to focus on specific parts of a system instead of understanding the complex interdependencies between them (Sterman, 2000). And that's where systems thinking comes in: a way of viewing the world as interconnected systems and considering their interactions, instead of just the components in isolation (Meadows, 2009). Applying systems thinking to product design can help you foresee challenges and understand unexpected results, creating better products.

In this section, we will:

1. Discuss the concept of systems thinking

2. Understand why it is crucial for product design and management

3. Explore tools and strategies for applying systems thinking to your work

4. Provide practical advice and real-life examples

What is systems thinking?

In its simplest form, systems thinking is a discipline for seeing the "big picture" (Meadows, 2009). It involves understanding how complex systems—whether they are biological, social, or organizational—have interconnected external and internal elements. Systems thinking is founded on principles like change over time, feedback loops, and adaptation.

For product managers, applying systems thinking means recognizing that products exist within a broader context, extending beyond the technology or functions it provides. It means understanding your users, their needs and their environment, as well as the factors that influence decision-making and user adoption.

Why is systems thinking important for product design?

In an era of rapid technological change, competitive markets and diverse user needs, products that take a systems approach to problem-solving will have a better chance at succeeding. Some key reasons why systems thinking is valuable for product design and management include (Arnold & Wade, 2015):

1. Addressing real-world complexities: Systems thinking aims to identify and consider potential challenges, assumptions, and hidden variables as part of the design process.

2. Enhancing creativity and innovation: By taking a holistic view, new opportunities to create value and novel solutions may emerge.

3. Increasing resilience: Systems thinking helps detect vulnerabilities and sources of failure, which can inform strategies to strengthen and safeguard products.

Tools and strategies for systems thinking

A practical way to get started with systems thinking is to adopt different mental models, tools, and strategies that will help you analyze and understand complex systems. Here are some tools and methods that can aid in bringing systems thinking into your product design process:

1. Causal loop diagrams: A visual representation of essential variables and their interconnected relationships within a system. This tool can help product managers map out key feedback loops and understand how changes in one variable may affect others (Kim, 1992).

2. Stock and flow diagrams: These diagrams help visualize different "stocks" in a system, the "flows" between them, and how they change over time. This is especially useful for understanding resource constraints and designing products that can adapt to variable conditions (Sterman, 2000).

3. Scenario planning: A method that explores multiple possible futures, often based on different combinations of drivers or assumptions (Schoemaker, 1995). This can help you understand the range of potential system-level impacts and design more resilient products.

Furthermore, fostering a culture of system thinking within your team will also contribute to better product design. Encourage curiosity, empathy, and reflection. Openly discuss the assumptions you're working with, and be open to changing your mind when new information surfaces. Collaboration with other disciplines, such as data analysts or anthropologists, can also help bring new perspectives to your approach to product design.

Practical advice and real-life example

To illustrate the value of systems thinking and how it can influence product design, consider the story of the London Underground's Victoria Line opening in 1968. Initially, the demand for this line was underestimated, and passengers were faced with overcrowded trains and long waiting times during peak hours. Recognizing that the problem was not the size of the trains but the frequency in which they could run, the management introduced "skip-stop" scheduling to improve the capacity (Bayley, 2009). Instead of focusing on a singular element (e.g., larger trains), the decision-makers applied systems thinking to address the broader issue (the entire train system).

As a product manager, this example serves as a reminder to think beyond the immediate and seemingly obvious solutions. Ask yourself:

- How can we ensure we understand the broader context in which our product operates?

- In what ways might our product changes ripple through other connected systems?

In conclusion, incorporating systems thinking into your approach to product design can help identify hidden challenges, uncover innovative solutions, and design products that can adapt and thrive in complex environments. Embrace the interconnectedness of systems, develop mental models, and foster a culture of systemic inquiry within your team. By doing so, you'll not only accomplish your product goals but also become a stronger product manager.

6.3 Service Design and Ecosystem Mapping

As product management experts, we have to continually navigate complex and evolving business environments. One of the most critical aspects of our profession is the ability to understand our product/service ecosystem and optimize the design to ensure its success. In this section, we will delve into the concepts of service design and ecosystem mapping to help you, as a product manager, harness these essential skills in your journey to becoming a stronger product manager.

Service design is a multidisciplinary approach to understanding, creating, and delivering value through an organization's services. It focuses on the holistic user experience, from the early-stage research to the final touchpoints with users (Stickdorn, Hormess, Lawrence, & Schneider, 2018). This holistic approach allows product managers to ensure that their product/service not only resonates with users but also achieves its intended impact in the ecosystem it operates in.

Ecosystem mapping is a valuable technique that allows product managers to create a visual representation of their product's underlying systems, stakeholders, and relationships. This exercise presents an opportunity to understand the web of interdependencies and potential impact points of the product/service being offered. Wyder et al. (2021) describe an ecosystem mapping framework that outlines five dimensions: products, channels, end-users, stakeholders, and relationships. By clearly defining these dimensions, product managers can unearth new perspectives and identify ways to optimize their service design.

Now that we have a foundational understanding of these concepts, let's explore some practical advice and deep insights to apply them in your product management journey.

Practice Empathy –

Actively engaging with your users' needs and preferences is the cornerstone of any successful service design. Service design thinking emphasizes the importance of empathy interviews and user journey mapping as indispensable tools for gaining deep insights into users' worlds. Including emotional elements in your maps can reveal powerful connections and opportunities for product innovation (Stickdorn et al., 2018). Empathy should also extend beyond users to the entire ecosystem, including various stakeholders and partners; understanding their motivations will be invaluable for fostering healthy relationships within your product's environment.

Deep insight: Prioritize human-centric design over technology-centric solutions. A product/service that resonates with users on an emotional level will foster a loyal and engaged user base.

Collaborate Across Disciplines –

Service design does not happen in isolation. It is a multidisciplinary endeavor that requires input from various fields, including design, anthropology, psychology, and business strategy. By integrating perspectives from diverse stakeholders, you can create a more robust service blueprint that maps potential pain points, interactions, and opportunities for improvement (Stickdorn et al., 2018). Foster an inclusive culture that encourages collaboration and the exchange of ideas, allowing your service design strategy to be innovative and resilient in the face of change.

Deep insight: Encourage cross-functional team collaboration from the initial stages of your service design project. Sharing insights and expertise with colleagues can help identify blind spots and create a more holistic understanding of your ecosystem.

Experiment and Iterate –

Service design is an iterative process that continually evolves over time. Failure is an inherent aspect of innovation, so embracing a learning mindset allows you to gain valuable information from your mistakes (Wyder et al., 2021). Design thinking promotes rapid prototyping and early user testing, allowing product managers to quickly validate their ideas and adjust their service design accordingly. By continually refining your product/service, you can ensure that it remains relevant and competitive within its ecosystem.

Practical advice: Allocate time and resources to pilot different aspects of your service design before implementing it on a larger scale. By identifying areas for improvement early on, you can save valuable resources and maintain the overall project timeline.

Reflect and Adapt – The ecosystems in which products/services reside are dynamic and ever-changing. Regularly reviewing and updating your ecosystem maps will allow you to identify new trends, technologies, and strategic partnerships (Wyder et al., 2021). Continually monitoring changes in the landscape and adapting your service design in response will help you remain agile and resilient as a product manager.

Practical advice: Schedule periodic reviews of your ecosystem maps with cross-functional teams, including key stakeholders. This practice will enable you to realign priorities, identify new opportunities, and course-correct when needed.

By embracing service design and ecosystem mapping, you will be in a stronger position to navigate the complexities of your product management role. These essential skills enable product managers to understand their users, collaborate more effectively, and flexibly adapt to the ever-changing business environment. Equipped with these tools and insights, you will be well on your way to becoming a stronger product manager.

6.4 Applying Lean Startup Principles

As a product manager, you may have heard about the growing prominence of the Lean Startup movement, first introduced by Eric Ries in 2011. This groundbreaking approach to business and innovation has been praised for its effectiveness in reducing risk and uncertainty while optimizing innovative processes (Ries, 2011). But what does it mean to apply Lean principles to product management, and how can you integrate these methodologies into your professional practice? In this section, we will explore the insights and implications of Lean methodologies for product management, supplemented by research in the field and practical advice.

First, let's briefly review the core components of the Lean Startup approach. According to Ries (2011), the fundamental idea of Lean Startup is to develop a Minimum Viable Product (MVP) to test a product hypothesis and then iterate based on feedback from real customers. The core components of the lean startup approach are the Build-Measure-Learn loop and the notion of "pivoting" or changing directions when evidence suggests the original idea may not be successful or scalable.

To apply these principles to product management, consider implementing the following steps:

Define your product hypothesis: To practice Lean methodology in product management, begin by formulating a clear and testable hypothesis regarding your target customers' needs and your product's potential to address these needs (Blank & Dorf, 2012). This hypothesis will act as the foundation for your product development process and inform the goals of your MVP.

Develop an MVP: In the Lean approach, the MVP serves as an initial, stripped-down version of a product designed to test the validity of your product hypothesis (Ries, 2011). When crafting your MVP, focus on developing a simplified version of your envisioned product that will provide enough value to your target customers while minimizing time and resources spent in the development process.

Test the MVP with real customers: Once your MVP is ready, release it to a small, representative group of your target audience. This is an essential step, as it grounds your product development process in real-world feedback and ensures you're building a product that truly addresses customer needs (Ries, 2011). Monitor customer interactions with the MVP closely and collect feedback, paying particular attention to any unexpected outcomes or difficulties users encounter.

Iterate and pivot as needed: Use the feedback gathered during the MVP testing to refine your product hypothesis, adjust your development goals, and devise a plan for improving the product (Maurya, 2012). Depending on the severity of the issues uncovered, you may decide to pivot your product direction entirely or refine the existing product.

Rinse and repeat: Once you've made the necessary changes to your product based on customer feedback, it's time to rebuild, retest, and iterate again. The Lean Startup method emphasizes continual learning and improvement throughout the entire product development process (Ries, 2011), so don't be afraid to repeat these steps multiple times before launching a final version.

By consistently adhering to the principles of the Lean Startup methodology, product managers can accelerate learning, minimize wasted resources, and ultimately build products that better serve customers' needs. In fact, research by Davidsson et al. (2016) has shown that the use of Lean Startup methods in the early stages of product development lead to improved organizational performance and increased chances of product success.

Moreover, Lean Startup methods provide another essential advantage for product managers: agility. In an increasingly dynamic and competitive marketplace, the ability to rapidly respond to shifting customer needs and preferences is critical for success. Product managers who embrace Lean Startup principles are better positioned to adapt and pivot quickly, ensuring their products remain at the cutting edge of their industry (Ries, 2011).

In conclusion, the Lean Startup methodology offers a valuable framework for product managers seeking to reduce risk and uncertainty while maximizing their ability to develop successful, customer-centric products. Integrating this mindset and practices into your product management approach will not only improve the development process but provide you and your team with the agile, customer-focused mentality needed in today's competitive marketplace.

Chapter 7: Product Execution and Process Management

Hello there, fellow product managers! As you've navigated through the previous sections of our journey into becoming stronger product managers, you've read about vision, strategy, and creating delightful user experiences. However, even with the best visions in mind, even the most well-crafted strategies or the most splendid UX designs, a product may still fall short if it's not executed and managed effectively.

That's where product execution and process management come into play. If you're wondering how you can effectively execute your product and manage processes, look no further. Buckle up and join me as we dive into the world of execution and process management, where we'll explore the key elements of successful product execution, the importance of staying adaptable, and everything in between.

Let's start by grasping this key piece of insight: Effective product execution and process management are major determinants of a product's success or failure (Thompson & Martin, 2010). While ideas are important, it's the execution that brings those ideas to life, establishes their value, and draws in your customers.

So, let's dive into what it takes to make your product execution sing.

1. Prioritizing Tasks and Features

One common challenge that product managers face is deciding which tasks and features should take priority (Cohen, 2018). While it's tempting to try and cram as many features as possible into a product, it's crucial to strike the right balance by identifying those that will drive the right outcomes for customers and the business.

Use a prioritization framework to help make these tough decisions. Some popular frameworks include the RICE model (Reach, Impact, Confidence, and Effort), the Kano Model, and MoSCoW method (Must-have, Should-have, Could-have, and Won't-have). Remember, the key here is to focus on delivering value, not just chasing down technological advancements or new trends.

2. Set Realistic Goals and Deadlines

As a product manager, you're often balancing a multitude of factors and stakeholders when determining release dates and deadlines (Chaudhary, 2016). While it's essential to work efficiently and release updates in a timely fashion, it's equally important to avoid setting unrealistic deadlines. This can lead to crunch or burnout, affecting team morale and, ultimately, product quality.

To avoid setting unrealistic deadlines, follow these steps:

- Break down tasks into smaller, more manageable pieces.

- Estimate the time required for each task, with input from all stakeholders.

- Factor in any dependencies and potential delays.

- Always add buffers for unforeseen challenges or changes in scope.

3. Communicate and Collaborate Effectively

A key aspect of product execution and process management lies in effective communication and collaboration among team members, particularly in cross-functional teams. Foster an environment of openness, trust, and accountability. Use tools like Asana, Trello, or Basecamp for task management; Slack, Microsoft Teams, or Google Hangouts for communication; and Confluence, Quip, or OneNote for team collaboration.

Remember that part of collaboration involves encouraging team members to voice their concerns or share updates regularly, so don't hesitate to ask for their thoughts and input. This not only promotes a positive culture but can also help uncover new opportunities or expose potential threats.

4. Continuously Evaluate and Adapt

Product execution and process management is not a one-time exercise but requires learning and adapting over time. Establish a feedback loop that allows for collecting, understanding, and incorporating learnings from various sources, such as user feedback, market research, and internal reviews.

Regular reviews and retrospectives can uncover ways to improve processes, resolve bottlenecks, and ultimately, deliver better products more efficiently. Additionally, adapt your process based on the changing needs of your product, team, or environment; staying agile and responsive can help you stay ahead of the game.

To sum it up, effective product execution and process management involve prioritizing features, setting realistic goals, fostering collaboration, and continuous evaluation and adaptation. By internalizing these principles and integrating them into your day-to-day activities, you can unlock the full potential of your product vision and strategy, leading to long-term success and growth.

So go forth, fearless product manager, and let these deep insights be your guiding light as you bring your innovative ideas and ambitious visions to life.

7.1 Agile methodologies for effective product execution

As a product manager, staying ahead in the ever-changing landscape of technology and markets requires a consistent and efficient way of handling product development. In fact, high-performing organizations are 1.7 times more likely to use agile methodologies in their projects (VersionOne, 2017). Utilizing agile methodologies is a proven way to not only keep up but thrive in this fast-paced environment. In this section, I will share some insights and practical advice about implementing agile methodologies to help you create and deliver better products, faster.

Agile methodologies emerged in response to the realization that traditional, waterfall-oriented approaches to product development were too slow and unwieldy for modern-day products, resulting in an inability to adapt quickly (Dingsøyr, Nerur, Balijepally, & Moe, 2018). This exposed a need to pivot and respond promptly, which led to the concept of agile being born. Agile methodologies are centered on iterative and incremental development, enabling product teams to collaborate closely and deliver frequent, smaller updates aligned with customer needs.

Here are a few key principles of agile methodologies that will help you create more effective processes around your product execution:

Prioritize customer satisfaction through continuous delivery: One of the core tenets of agile philosophy is to prioritize customer needs by delivering valuable software frequently and consistently. Conversations with stakeholders and customers should be a constant process, ensuring the backlog remains up-to-date with the latest insights and feedback. By doing this, your team will know they are focusing on the right features and improvements, maximizing your product's appeal to the target audience.

Embrace change, even late in development: Contrary to traditional methodologies, agile encourages effective planning to accommodate changes at any stage in the lifecycle. Your ability to adapt to shifting market demands or new competition will ultimately determine the success of your product. Be willing to revise priorities and scope with minimal disruption to the overall goals as new information arises.

Build cross-functional, self-organizing teams: Agile relies on highly collaborative, self-organizing teams that house a diverse set of skills and expertise (Pertiller, 2019). Encourage your team to take ownership of their work and the success of the product, fostering a culture of continuous improvement and personal development. Invest in regular training and team-building initiatives to maintain optimal performance levels within your team.

Measure success through working software: One of the most valuable outcomes of agile development is the ability to ship working products incrementally. Establish a robust definition of the "minimum viable product" (MVP) and iterate from there, with regularly scheduled releases that add value to the customer. This will enable your team to receive feedback and make informed decisions about the next steps in the development process.

Maintain a sustainable pace: Agile emphasizes the importance of maintaining a steady, sustainable pace throughout the entire process. Encourage your team to iterate and improve upon their own practices, rather than burning out from a mad dash to meet deadlines. Strike a balance between speed and quality to ensure long-term success.

Now that you're familiar with the core principles of agile methodologies, let's discuss two deep insights that can take your product execution to the next level:

Create a product-centric, rather than a project-centric, culture: To truly embrace the agile philosophy, your organization must shift its focus from project-based activities toward nurturing and growing products over their entire lifecycle. Cultivating cross-functional, long-lived product teams that work together from ideation through to maintenance and sunsetting can significantly reduce overheads, improve product quality and accelerate innovation (Leoni, Oppici, & Rossi, 2018).

Align the organization around agile principles: Although adopting agile methodologies has shown great success within product development teams, the most significant benefits will arise when the entire organization embraces agile principles. Collaborate across departments to create an end-to-end agile process that spans from marketing and sales through to product delivery and customer support. This approach will result in a more unified, cohesive organization and enable the creation of extraordinary products that delight users consistently.

By understanding and leveraging agile methodologies, you can support your team in becoming more flexible, results-oriented, and responsive to customers' needs. This approach not only ensures the delivery of cutting-edge products that your customers will love but also prepares your product development organization for the challenges and opportunities of today and tomorrow.

7.2 Setting up Efficient Product Processes

As a product manager, one of the most crucial aspects of your job is to establish efficient product processes that keep your team on track and deliver successful products. In this chapter, we will delve into the various ways you can set up efficient product processes to create well-crafted, customer-focused products.

It is essential to acknowledge that no process is one-size-fits-all. What works for one team or product may not work for another. In order to develop a system that is right for your team, you must first understand the variety of processes that are available and be willing to adapt as needed. After all, flexibility and adaptability are at the core of successful product management.

Streamline Your Processes

When an organization is bogged down with unnecessary steps and complexities, it can become a barrier to innovation and collaboration. According to a study by Harvard Business Review (Fleming & Sorenson, 2013) on bureaucracy, bureaucratic procedures can accumulate like sediment over time, causing organizations to become less adaptable and less efficient.

To combat this phenomenon, it is essential to look for ways to streamline and clarify your process. For instance, reconsider any steps that do not add significant value to your product or your team's overall goals. You may also examine how similar teams have simplified their processes and identify areas where you can follow suit.

Build a Strong Team Culture

A collaborative and supportive team is the backbone of any successful product process. Research by Forrester Consulting (2020) found that "fostering a strong team culture is the top reason for adopting Agile practices," and it can even lead to faster product development, better resource allocation, and increased innovation.

You can build a strong team culture by establishing a clear vision and providing opportunities for open communication, thereby fostering trust and mutual understanding among team members. Moreover, don't forget to celebrate your team's wins and address any challenges head-on.

Make Data-Driven Decisions

Another crucial aspect of efficient product processes is leveraging data to inform your decision-making. In a McKinsey report (Reill & Plechinger, 2017), researchers found that companies taking an increased hands-on approach to managing data can gain significant competitive advantages.

By using data and analytics to reduce time-to-market, optimize features, and validate your product-market fit, you can ensure your team and product are on the right track. Moreover, establish a robust feedback loop with ample room to accommodate improvements based on customer feedback and usage data.

Embrace Agile Methodologies

Agile methodologies can be a game-changer for setting up efficient product processes. According to the State of Agile Report (2020), 95% of organizations are using Agile practices, and 58% of respondents credit Agile for better project visibility.

By creating cross-functional teams, encouraging frequent communication, setting iterative goals, and prioritizing customer feedback, Agile methodologies can help your team develop a more adaptable, responsive, and efficient product process.

Establish Clear and Transparent Responsibilities

Confusion and overlapping responsibilities can cause a product team to lose precious time and resources. By delineating clear roles and responsibilities, you ensure that every team member knows what is expected of them and how they contribute to the overall product process.

This clarity will empower team members to execute their tasks effectively and confidently, ultimately leading to better product outcomes and a more efficient process overall.

Deep Insight #1 - Foster Innovation and Flexibility

By adopting an environment that encourages innovation and flexibility, your team can test new concepts, explore creative solutions, and iterate in ways that lead to more effective product processes. Encourage your team members to challenge the status quo, propose new ideas, and explore unconventional methods.

Deep Insight #2 - Never Stop Learning

The world of product management is constantly evolving, with emerging technologies and methodologies shaping the industry. To stay ahead of the curve, it is crucial to embrace lifelong learning and actively seek new technologies, best practices, and product management strategies that could optimize your process efficiency.

In conclusion, setting up efficient product processes involves a combination of streamlining processes, building a strong team culture, leveraging data, adopting Agile methodologies, and establishing clear roles and responsibilities. Adopt an environment that fosters innovation and flexibility, and never stop learning to continuously improve and optimize your product management processes.

7.3 Managing Product Backlogs and Prioritization

As a product manager, one of your most important tasks is to ensure the product backlog is well-organized, prioritized, and maintained. The product backlog is a living document that contains everything you want to add or change in your product. The list can have various items such as features, bug fixes, improvements, and technical debt. As the project progresses, the backlog becomes more challenging to manage and prioritize. That's why we have dedicated this section to provide you with practical advice and insights on how to manage your product backlog and prioritize items effectively.

Understanding the importance of a well-managed product backlog

A product backlog lays the foundation for product development (Cohen, 2020). Without a well-structured backlog, projects can quickly go off track and lose focus. Managing the product backlog allows you to:

1. Keep track of all product requirements and tasks.

2. Prioritize tasks based on their business value and dependencies.

3. Align your team's efforts with the project's objectives.

4. Communicate the project's status and direction to stakeholders.

5. Analyze and measure the progress made towards the project's goals.

Setting up your product backlog

Before diving into prioritization, it's essential to ensure your product backlog is well-structured and easy to navigate. To achieve this, follow these steps:

1. Create a single, central repository: Having one source of truth makes it easy for the team to access, update, and review the backlog (Lehtonen, 2021).

2. Categorize backlog items: Divide the backlog into categories such as features, bugs, improvements, and technical debt. Assigning labels or using color coding can make items easily distinguishable.

3. Write clear and concise descriptions: Each item in the backlog should have a well-defined description that explains what it is and how it will benefit the product or users.

4. Estimate effort and value: Assign effort points to each backlog item to indicate its complexity and potential value to the product (e.g., using story points).

Prioritizing the product backlog

Now that you have an organized backlog, it's time to prioritize its items. Prioritizing a product backlog ensures that the most valuable work items are addressed first, creating a clear path towards your project's goals. Below are some prioritization techniques to help you make those crucial decisions:

1. *MoSCoW Method:* Categorize backlog items into four buckets – Must-have, Should-have, Could-have, and Won't-have. This method allows you to quickly identify high-priority tasks and focus on them (Reinertsen, 2009).

2. *Value vs. Effort Matrix:* Draw a matrix with two axes – value and effort. Place items in the matrix based on their perceived value to the business and the estimated effort to complete the task. Focus on high value, low effort items first.

3. *Weighted Shortest Job First (WSJF):* Calculate the WSJF score for each item by dividing its Cost of Delay (value) by the effort required. The higher the score, the higher the priority.

Two deep insights on managing product backlogs and prioritization

1. Embrace uncertainty: Change is inevitable in product management. Embrace changes to your backlog and continuously reassess priorities as you receive new information or feedback (Cohen, 2020). This approach will help you keep your product development agile and adapt to evolving requirements.

2. Collaborate with stakeholders: The product backlog affects many stakeholders, including developers, designers, marketing, sales, and customers. Involve them in the prioritization process to generate diverse perspectives and better understand their needs (Lehtonen, 2021). Their inputs can lead to more accurate prioritization and a balanced product roadmap.

Managing a product backlog and prioritizing its items are critical aspects of product management. A well-structured backlog eases your prioritization efforts, while effective prioritization ensures that valuable items are addressed first. By embracing change and collaborating with stakeholders, you can better adapt to changing requirements and make data-driven decisions that drive your product towards success.

7.4 Balancing Short-Term Gains with Long-Term Objectives

one key challenge you'll encounter is striking the right balance between short-term gains and long-term objectives. Falling into the trap of focusing solely on quick wins can put your product's long-term success at risk. On the other hand, obsessing over long-term goals without delivering value in the short term can frustrate your customers and stakeholders. In this section, we'll explore how to navigate this balance, drawing from research and practical advice to help you become a stronger product manager.

First and foremost, it's crucial to understand why balancing short-term gains and long-term objectives is so important. A study by Harvard Business School professor, Clay Christensen, emphasizes that companies that focus exclusively on short-term financial performance ultimately underperform those that invest in long-term growth (Christensen, 2012). The research suggests that overlooking long-term objectives may yield temporary success but can lead to failure in the end.

To better understand this balance, it's helpful to recognize the differences between the two perspectives. Short-term gains involve a focus on immediate returns, often achieved through quick fixes, cost-cutting, and efficiency improvements. Long-term objectives, however, center around a product's strategic vision and involve innovation, customer retention, and sustainable growth.

Now that we've established the importance of this balance and its underlying components, let's dive into some practical advice for managing this tightrope as a product manager.

1. Set clear priorities:

Begin by defining your priorities for both short-term gains and long-term objectives. By clearly outlining the key targets for each time frame, you'll ensure that both perspectives are duly represented in your decision-making and avoid inadvertently skewed priorities (Sirkin et al., 2005).

2. Develop a product roadmap:

A product roadmap can be an incredibly useful tool in striking this balance. By visually representing your product's development timeline, you'll provide a clear overview of short-term plans and their alignment with your long-term objectives.

3. Balance stakeholder interests:

As a product manager, you'll need to satisfy customers, external partners, and internal stakeholders. Understand what each group values and keep their needs in mind when deciding between short-term gains and long-term objectives. Strive for solutions that meet multiple parties' needs without sacrificing long-term success (Ojasalo, 2001).

4. Measure and evaluate success:

Create a set of key performance indicators (KPIs) to measure your progress towards short-term gains and long-term objectives. Regularly tracking and evaluating these metrics will allow you to adjust your strategies as needed, ensuring continued alignment with both perspectives.

5. Foster a culture of innovation:

Long-term objectives often require innovative thinking and a willingness to take calculated risks. Foster a culture that encourages these behaviors, providing both time and resources for longer-term endeavors.

Deep Insight #1 - Embrace the "innovation ambidexterity":

A study by O'Reilly and Tushman (2008) introduced the concept of "innovation ambidexterity" as the ability to balance exploration and exploitation. They concluded that companies that can successfully execute incremental innovation (exploitation) while pursuing breakthrough innovation (exploration) are more likely to achieve long-term success. As a product manager, it's critical to adopt this mindset, valuing both short-term gains and long-term objectives in parallel.

Deep Insight #2 - Adopt the "both/and" mindset:

The challenge of balancing short-term gains with long-term objectives often feels like an either/or decision. But embracing the "both/and" mindset can help you navigate this tension (Smith & Lewis, 2011). This perspective involves recognizing that short-term gains and long-term objectives are not mutually exclusive, and that trade-offs can be made in favor of both. Identify opportunities where you can achieve short-term gains while simultaneously moving closer to your long-term objectives.

In conclusion, balancing short-term gains with long-term objectives is a delicate and essential task for product managers. By applying the aforementioned practical advice, and always keeping the long-term goals in mind, you will set the stage for a successful and sustainable product.

Chapter 8: Personalization and Customization in Product Design

As a product manager, it's crucial to remember that your users are not a monolithic entity. People come from diverse backgrounds, have differing preferences, and varying skill levels. One-size-fits-all products no longer work as effectively as they used to. Enter personalization and customization in product design, which aims to give users more control over their experiences, while also tailoring the product to suit their specific needs and preferences.

In this chapter, we will discuss the importance of personalization and customization in product design, explore its benefits, and share some practical tips on how to implement personalized and customized experiences for your users. Drawing from research and real-life examples, we will also provide deep insights into the true power of these concepts.

Personalization vs. Customization

Before we dive into the topic, let's make an essential distinction: personalization and customization are not the same thing. Personalization is a highly targeted approach that tailors the user experience based on an individual's behaviors, preferences, and context. It typically happens automatically and dynamically, without any conscious effort from the user (Kumar & Reinartz, 2016).

On the other hand, customization requires active involvement from the user. They make selections or adjustments to the product or service to adapt it to their specific needs or preferences (Resnick & Varian, 1997). For example, personalization might display recommendations based on the user's browsing history, while customization allows the user to choose among different settings or options.

Deep Insight #1: The Balance of Control

Striking the right balance between personalization and customization is an art in itself. In a world of information overload, users appreciate and benefit from personalized experiences that reduce cognitive load and quickly present them with useful, relevant content. However, it's essential not to be too intrusive or limit user control, as people may get frustrated with recommendations or changes that they cannot adjust to their liking.

A study published in the Journal of Management Information Systems suggests that users appreciate personalization and find it helpful, but only when they trust that the system has their best interests in mind (Awad & Krishnan, 2006). This implies that an effective product should allow users to have a certain level of control over their experience, which is where customization comes into play.

Practical Advice #1: Combine Personalization and Customization for Optimal User Experiences

Leveraging personalization and customization together can yield powerful results. Personalization serves to create an initial connection between your product and a user's unique needs or preferences. Customization then allows them to fine-tune this experience, ensuring it feels truly their own.

One example can be seen in streaming services like Spotify, which combines both elements. Users receive personalized playlists based on their listening history and can further customize these by adding, removing, or reordering songs. Integrating customization features after providing a personalized experience can leave users feeling more satisfied and engaged.

Deep Insight #2: The Need for Transparent Algorithms

Personalization often relies on complex algorithms to make calculated suggestions, but users may feel uneasy about how these decisions are made. The 'black box' nature of many personalization algorithms might create mistrust and even cause users to reject the system entirely (Ribeiro, Singh, & Guestrin, 2016).

To alleviate this issue, it's essential to maintain transparency in your product's personalization features. Communicate how your algorithms work, why they're making specific recommendations, and create settings allowing users to adjust or tweak their personalization experiences.

Practical Advice #2: Build Trust Through Design

To ensure your users trust your personalization attempts, incorporate several strategies:

1. Be transparent about the data you're using and how you're using it. Make privacy policies clear and easily accessible.

2. Allow users to quickly edit or remove personalization preferences at any time.

3. Be mindful of 'creepy' recommendations – avoid sharing insights about the user that may be seen as invasive or border on personal surveillance.

4. Gradually introduce personalization features and allow users to become accustomed to them over time.

Personalization and customization are incredibly powerful tools in the product manager's arsenal. By understanding their nuances and implementing their synergies effectively, you can create truly engaging and satisfying experiences for your users. Keep in mind the importance of transparency and maintaining balance between user control and automation, and you'll be well on your way to crafting personalized and customized experiences that help your product stand out from the crowd.

8.1: Understanding Customer Needs and Preferences

Let's face it, your products and services are not inherently interesting. There, I said it. You might be passionate about them, but your customers are not. Your customers are not really interested in your products; they are interested in their own problems and how a product or service can make their lives better.

So, the dilemma every product manager faces is understanding customer needs and preferences – both stated and unstated. Learning to read between the lines and identifying what customers truly want can be transformative for any product manager. This chapter delves into the nuances of decoding customer needs and honing your skills as a product manager.

There are two types of customer needs: articulated needs (those customers can consciously express and easily put into words) and unarticulated needs (those customers may not even know they have). As a product manager, your ability to identify unarticulated needs can set your product apart in the marketplace. For instance, ten years ago, nobody explicitly said they wanted a smartphone with an app for everything. iPhone's success can be chalked up to its uncanny ability to meet unarticulated customer needs.

To understand your customers, you need to go beyond surveys, questionnaires, and focus groups. While these methods are useful for gathering articulated needs, they often fall short in capturing unarticulated needs (Olson & Bakke, 2001). This is where customer empathy comes into play.

Customer empathy is the ability to put yourself in your customers' shoes, understanding their problems and aspirations. It's an essential ingredient in product management, enabling you to see the world from your customer's perspective and identify the true value your product offers. Here are some practical methods for developing customer empathy:

Observation: The simplest way to understand customers is by watching them interact with your product or a similar one. Pay attention to their struggles, frustrations, and moments of delight. These observations can help you uncover unarticulated customer needs and guide product development.

Contextual Inquiry: Talk to your customers in their context – their homes, offices, or wherever they use your product. Observe them, ask questions, and understand the context in which your product operates (Holtzblatt & Beyer, 2013). This will help you glean insights into customers' lives that surveys cannot capture.

Empathy Mapping: Create an empathy map to help you visualize your customers' needs, preferences, and context. This can be a valuable tool in uncovering unarticulated needs and pain points.

Now that you're equipped to understand customer needs let's dive into the world of preferences. Customer preferences shape purchasing decisions and, ultimately, product success. They can be explicit, like a preference for a specific color, or implicit, like a preference for environmentally friendly products.

Here are some practical tips to understand and shape customer preferences:

1. Segment your customers: All customers are not alike, and their preferences vary. Group customers with similar preferences and address their needs to maximize your product's appeal to the target market.

2. Influence preferences through branding: Your brand has the power to shape customer preferences. A strong brand can evoke positive associations and

build trust, ultimately driving customer preferences in your favor (Keller, 1993).

3. Design to delight: Use principles of design thinking to make your product intuitive, easy to use, and delightful to look at. This can go a long way in shaping customer preferences in your favor.

Finally, it's important to note that customer needs and preferences can change faster than ever in today's fast-paced world. As a product manager, it's essential to stay agile and adapt to these changes. Keep a close eye on emerging trends, competitor moves, and market shifts. Regularly update your customer empathy skills and understanding of customer needs and preferences to remain ahead of the curve.

In a nutshell, understanding customer needs and preferences is of utmost importance for product managers. By developing customer empathy and adapting to changing needs and preferences, you can ensure your product resonates with its target audience and becomes a success.

Now that you've got the basics down, let's move on to the next chapter, where we'll discuss how to test and validate your product ideas using customer feedback.

8.2 Techniques for Creating Personalized Experiences

Personalization has become a fundamental aspect of product management in recent years. When done effectively, personalization in products and services can create immense value, improve user experience, and foster customer loyalty. In fact, a study by Epsilon found that 80% of consumers are more likely to make a purchase when brands offer personalized experiences (Roberts & Berger, 2018). But how can product managers create such experiences to enhance the value of the products they oversee? In this section, we'll explore several techniques that can be used to create personalized experiences and provide practical advice on implementing these strategies.

Understand your users through data:

The first step in creating personalized experiences is to get to know your users. Collecting and analyzing user data allows you to understand their preferences, habits, demographics, and goals. This information can then be used to tailor your product's features and services according to the needs of individual users. Several analytical tools can be employed for this purpose, including Google Analytics, Mixpanel, and Amplitude (Ward, 2018). Data-driven personalization promotes a better understanding of users' needs, resulting in improved user experiences and increased engagement.

Deep Insight: User research should be an ongoing process, as users' needs and preferences will likely change over time. Keep track of the trends and constantly analyze user data to ensure that your product continues to offer personalized experiences that cater to the evolving requirements of your audience.

Utilize machine learning and AI:

Advances in technology have provided product managers with the ability to leverage machine learning and artificial intelligence (AI) to create highly effective personalized experiences. By processing vast amounts of data rapidly, AI can identify patterns and correlations that may not be apparent to humans, providing deeper insights into user behavior (Levy & Stone, 2019). Machine learning algorithms can be used to recommend products, services or content that are highly relevant to individual users, based on their past behavior and preferences. Companies like Netflix, Amazon, and Spotify are already successfully implementing these technologies to tailor their offerings to users' tastes.

Deep Insight: The true potential of AI-powered personalization lies in moving beyond simple recommendations to highly contextual interactions. Using AI to understand the exact moment when a particular recommendation or feature could be most useful to a user, and offering it precisely then, can significantly enhance user experience.

Segmentation and targeted messaging:

Grouping your users based on shared characteristics (e.g., age, location, interests) allows you to deliver more relevant and personalized content or marketing messages. Creating segments based on user data and employing targeted messaging can lead to increased user engagement and conversion rates. For example, sending targeted promotional offers to users who have abandoned their shopping carts can encourage them to complete their purchases (Moorthy et al., 2020).

Practical Advice: Make sure to regularly review and adjust your segmentation criteria to maintain optimal user targeting. Investing in automation tools for targeted messaging can improve the efficiency of your personalization efforts.

A/B testing and optimization:

Once you've implemented personalized experiences in your product, A/B testing is crucial to determine which personalized strategies work best for your users. A/B testing involves comparing two different versions of a feature, design, or marketing approach to see which yields better results in terms of user engagement and satisfaction. Constantly testing and optimizing your personalization efforts ensures that your strategies remain effective and relevant to users' needs (Kohavi et al., 2013).

Practical Advice: Develop a continuous improvement mindset, and don't be afraid to iterate and optimize your personalized experiences based on the results of your A/B tests. Keep the focus on your users and be willing to adapt to their ever-changing preferences.

By employing these techniques and fostering a deep understanding of your users, you can create personalized experiences that truly resonate with your audience. Moreover, with the help of data analytics, AI-assisted recommendations, segmentation, and A/B testing, product managers can better serve their users, leading to increased user satisfaction, engagement, and ultimately, business success.

8.3 The Role of AI in Personalization and Customization

As a product manager, understanding the nuances of personalization and customization has become increasingly important in this era of Artificial Intelligence (AI) advancements. Most importantly, differentiating between personalization and customization is integral in delivering an optimized user experience. To provide some clarity, personalization involves using AI and algorithms to automatically offer tailored experiences based on user behavior or data provided, while customization allows users to adjust the product directly to suit their preferences (Toubia et al., 2017). The appropriate balance of both elements can significantly enhance user satisfaction and product adoption.

The power of AI can significantly aid product managers in delivering personalized experiences to users. In recent years, AI has revolutionized the way consumers interact with products and services, ranging from personalized recommendations on e-commerce sites to individually customized diets and health plans. Research suggests that AI's ability to predict and recommend products based on user data has been proven to increase user engagement by up to 21% (Yan et al., 2011).

An increasing number of businesses are also leveraging AI-powered chatbots to provide personalized customer support based on collected user data. Chatbots that learn from user interactions can offer improved customer experiences, as they adapt to each unique user's preferences, achieving a 40% increase in customer satisfaction ratings compared to chatbots that do not use AI (Xu et al., 2017). Thus, incorporating AI can enable companies to deliver highly personalized experiences that cater to user needs without the stress of manual customization.

One deep insight is to leverage AI to improve upon traditional recommendation and filtering algorithms. Implementing AI-driven models like collaborative filtering can help recommend relevant products or services to users by analyzing patterns in their behavior along with the behavior of others with similar interests. These models give product managers the ability to harness the user's implicit preferences instead of relying solely on their explicit inputs (Toubia et al., 2017). This not only streamlines the user experience but also provides a level of personalization that would be difficult to achieve with customization alone.

Another deep insight is that AI can also analyze user data to generate highly individualized content in real-time. By understanding a user's preferences, motivations, and psychographic traits, AI algorithms can assemble unique content that appeals to them on an individual level. Combining this with customization options allows users to further tailor the experience to their unique requirements. In some cases, like news websites or social media platforms, a careful balance of personalization and customization can help users see the value in the suggested content beyond what their own configurations can achieve (Toubia et al., 2017).

To achieve success in merging AI-powered personalization with customization, keep the following practical advice in mind:

1. Understand your users: Conduct thorough user research to get a good grasp of user habits,

preferences, motivations, and use cases. Identifying the variables that contribute to user satisfaction in your product category will enable you to optimize your AI algorithms and provide a more personalized experience based on those attributes.

2. Test and iterate: As AI learns from user interactions, it's essential to continuously test and improve your algorithms to ensure relevance and satisfaction. Monitor user feedback and conduct A/B testing on different personalization and customization strategies to identify the most effective balance for your unique offering.

3. Ensure transparency: When using AI for personalization, be transparent with your users about what data is being collected and how it is being used. Offering users the option to opt-out of certain forms of data collection and personalization can prevent feelings of intrusion and build trust in your product.

4. Combine personalization with customization: Although AI algorithms can provide highly personalized experiences, don't forget to include customization options for your users. By giving users control over their preferences, you'll enhance their satisfaction even further.

In conclusion, integrating AI into your product's personalization and customization strategies can drive increased user satisfaction and engagement. Understanding the appropriate balance between the two and continuously testing and refining algorithms will result in a more rewarding user experience and contribute to the overall success of your product. So, dear product managers, embrace the power of AI, and discover endless opportunities to delight your users through personalization and customization.

8.4 Balancing personalization with privacy concerns

As product managers, we are constantly searching for new and innovative ways to improve the user experience, anticipating their needs, and exceeding their expectations. Personalization is a powerful tool in achieving this goal, by tailoring the product experience to the preferences, habits, and desires of individual users (Peelen and Beltman, 2013). However, delivering a truly personalized experience often requires access to users' personal data, sparking privacy concerns and ethical dilemmas. Balancing personalization with privacy concerns is a critical skill for product managers in today's digital age.

Let's first understand the challenge. Personalization is a major driver of engagement and user satisfaction, with studies showing that personalized experiences can increase consumer spending by 500% and improve the effectiveness of marketing campaigns by up to 30% (Mitchell, 2021). On the other hand, privacy concerns are becoming increasingly important to users, fueled by high-profile data breaches and growing awareness of data mining practices. According to a PwC survey, 85% of consumers actively consider privacy when making purchasing decisions, and 64% have experienced at least one privacy-related incident in the past (PwC, 2020).

With these considerations in mind, how can product managers strike the right balance between personalization and privacy?

1. Be transparent and create trust

A key component of balancing personalization and privacy is fostering trust with your users. Make sure you are transparent about the data collected, how it is used, and the benefits users can expect by sharing their data. Create an easily accessible, clear, and concise privacy policy, and ensure users have the opportunity to review and adjust their privacy settings.

When changes are made to your data collection or usage practices, treat it as an opportunity to re-engage your users and remind them of the value they derive from personalization. By being upfront about the information we collect and how we use it, we can work to alleviate privacy concerns (Li, 2019).

2. Minimize data collection and storage

Respect your user's privacy by collecting only the data necessary to power personalization features. An easy way to determine this is by asking yourself this question: If you were to be asked by a customer to justify the collection of a specific data point, would you have a solid, user-benefiting answer?

Stay within the bounds of the "need-to-know" principle, collecting minimal personally identifiable information (PII), and utilizing anonymization techniques when possible (e.g., aggregation or tokenization of PII).

3. Empower user control over their data

Give your users control over the data they share with your service. Provide clear and easy-to-navigate options for adjusting their privacy settings, opting out of data sharing, or even deleting their data entirely. By giving users control over their data, you are not only protecting their privacy but also building trust and loyalty.

4. Establish strong data security measures

Implement robust data security measures to protect the information you do collect. Regularly review and update data protection practices and ensure that your team is educated on security best practices. Remember that security is not a one-time implementation but an ongoing process requiring continuous attention.

5. Collaborate with cross-functional teams

Ensure that privacy concerns are considered across all facets of product development. Work closely with your UX, engineering, and legal teams to create well-rounded solutions that balance personalization with privacy.

By following these guidelines, product managers can deliver personalized experiences that drive user satisfaction while also respecting and maintaining user privacy. The key lies in transparency, focusing on features with tangible benefits, and making it easy for users to control their data. With this balanced approach, we can not only deliver an exceptional product experience but also foster a relationship of trust with our users.

Chapter 9: The Use of AI in Product Management

Imagine a scenario where you're working with hundreds of customer feedback points, thousands of success metrics to track, and an overwhelming amount of ideas from your team to improve your product. As a product manager, this vast quantity of information makes it extremely challenging to quickly analyze and derive insights to guide your team in the right direction. Well, it's time to consider bringing a new member to your team, and that's artificial intelligence (AI).

In recent years, AI has revolutionized various industries and is poised to play a significant role in product management as well. AI has the potential to turn the tide in your favor by helping you make data-driven decisions, predict your customers' needs, and deliver timely improvements (Kumar & Sharma, 2020). In this section, we will discuss some practical applications of AI in product management and deep insights to help you stay one step ahead of the game.

1. **Harnessing the power of AI in customer feedback analysis**

Effective product management revolves around the needs and pain points of your customers. Traditionally, capturing, processing, and analyzing customer feedback has been a burdensome and time-consuming process (Nayak, 2020). However, with the advent of AI, you can easily and effectively analyze massive amounts of customer feedback data, such as product reviews, social media comments, and support tickets, to identify recurring themes, sentiment, and key insights about your product.

For instance, natural language processing (NLP), a branch of AI, can be used to automatically classify and analyze unstructured text data, while sentiment analysis can gauge customer emotions behind their feedback. By leveraging AI in this context, product managers can discover opportunities for improvement, identify trending issues, and uncover user expectations much faster than before.

Deep insight: To reap the full benefits of AI in customer feedback analysis, prioritize integrating AI-powered analysis tools into your existing feedback collection and analysis processes. This will empower you to find meaningful patterns and trends that traditional methods might overlook, and ultimately lead to well-informed, customer-centric decisions.

2. Revolutionizing product predictions and personalization

Another powerful application of AI in product management is its ability to recognize patterns and trends, and subsequently make predictions about customers' future actions and preferences (Kumar & Sharma, 2020). By analyzing historical data, customer behavior, and external influences like market trends or competitor activity, AI can predict outcomes such as user churn or demand for specific product features.

For example, AI algorithms can help product managers estimate the return on investment (ROI) associated with introducing a new feature, or predict which customers are more likely to convert into paying users. With this information, product managers can prioritize initiatives that have the maximum impact on their bottom line.

Furthermore, AI can be instrumental in personalizing each individual user's experience. Instead of a one-size-fits-all approach, you can tailor the user interface and recommendations to match each user's preferences, which can lead to higher satisfaction and engagement rates.

Deep insight: To leverage AI for product predictions and personalization, make sure your data gathering processes are robust and accurate. The quality of your predictions relies heavily on the quality of the data you collect, so investing in strong data pipelines and practices is essential for best results.

3. Optimizing workflows and decision-making with AI-powered tools

By applying AI to internal processes and decision-making, product managers can improve their team's efficiency and productivity. Activities like ideation, feature prioritization, testing, and release management can all benefit from AI's ability to process large amounts of data and provide insights in real-time.

One practical approach to using AI in decision-making is to utilize AI-powered project management tools that can allocate resources, suggest task prioritization, and highlight potential risks. For instance, AI can help product managers forecast completion dates for different work items and identify which tasks are the most crucial for meeting milestones.

Additionally, with the help of machine learning, AI can learn from the team's past decisions and outcomes, allowing it to make improved recommendations over time. By removing guesswork and human biases from the equation, AI-powered tools can significantly improve the quality of decisions made by the product team.

Finally, AI can also help automate repetitive tasks or routine processes, freeing your team to focus on higher-value activities related to product innovation and strategy.

Deep insight: To fully exploit the advantages of AI in optimizing workflows and decision-making, it's critical to maintain open communication and collaboration within your team. Keep in mind that AI is not a replacement for human intuition and creativity; instead, it's a powerful tool that complements your team's expertise, enabling them to make informed decisions in a more efficient manner.

Conclusion

The integration of AI in product management can transform the way you handle customer feedback, make predictions about your users, and optimize your workflows. By tapping into the power of AI, you'll not only become a stronger product manager, but also gain a competitive edge that helps to drive your product's success. Embrace this technology, and prepare to witness a significant improvement in your product management capabilities.

9.1 AI-powered Analytics and Insights

As a product manager, it's your responsibility to keep your fingers on the pulse of your product's performance and find ways to refine and improve it continually. One of the most significant advancements in recent years that's worth looking at is the implementation of artificial intelligence (AI) in product analytics. The AI-powered analytics landscape promises to provide massive benefits, such as efficiency, cost reductions, and better insights. In this chapter, we delve into the core facets of AI-powered analytics, their importance in product management, and practical advice on embracing AI as part of your decision-making arsenal.

Artificial intelligence has proven to be very effective in various sectors, such as healthcare, finance, and retail, providing business growth and more informed decision-making. A study by McKinsey Global Institute (2018) demonstrates the potential of AI in analyzing data related to user behavior, market trends, and competitors. Their research estimates that AI-powered analytics could add $9.5 trillion to $15.4 trillion to the global economy by 2030. Following this projection, it becomes essential for a product manager to grasp the concept of AI analytics and understand how it can benefit their product.

Deep Insight 1: Personalized Product Recommendations

One of the applications of AI in product management surrounds personalized recommendations for individual users. As described by Fürnkranz and Hüllermeier (2018), machine learning models are highly adept at capturing complex patterns in user preferences and identifying meaningful relationships between items. By using AI algorithms such as collaborative filtering or matrix factorization, you can tailor product offerings specifically to user preferences, boosting sales and customer satisfaction.

For a product manager, this personalized approach can be highly beneficial. For instance, if an AI system within your analytics tool identifies that customers who bought Product A are more likely to purchase Product B, you might consider offering a discounted bundle of the two products or create marketing campaigns targeting those who've bought Product A.

Practical Advice: To leverage AI-powered personalization, approach your data science team to integrate AI-backed algorithms within your product management tools. Explicitly instruct them to help you find patterns in user preferences, which can eventually be used for personalized recommendations.

Deep Insight 2: Predictive Analysis for Product Optimization

Another exciting facet of AI analytics is their potential to predict future trends and product performance in the market. A research paper by Koli and Pandey (2018) highlights the significance of AI-based predictive analytic models for decision-making in business. The power of predictive analysis can be harnessed to forecast future sales, identify the performance of a particular product category or even discover potential pitfalls before they escalate.

As a product manager, trusting AI-powered predictive analysis can yield beneficial results by allowing you to better prepare for fluctuations in market demands or predict the possible effects of an upcoming change in product features or design. Moreover, it allows you to optimize your product's overall roadmap by accurately forecasting its performance over time.

Practical Advice: Discuss the potential of employing predictive analysis with your data science team. Explore various AI-powered tools that can provide you with accurate predictions and market insights. By doing so, you can make well-informed decisions on the direction of your product, plan adjustments based on the forecasted performance, and adapt your product strategy accordingly.

Embracing AI-powered analytics and insights as part of your product management toolkit arms you with a valuable resource for driving your product's success. By using personalized recommendations and predictive analysis, you can position your offerings to cater better to your users' needs and preferences while planning product adjustments based on accurate forecasts of future performance.

In conclusion, investing in AI-powered analytics equips you as a product manager with a robust decision-making tool. Understanding the potential benefits of AI analytics is just the first step. Implementing, testing, and iterating until you develop a system tailored to your needs is where the actual challenge and opportunity lie. Don't hesitate to invest time and resources in this exciting new realm of analytics, and your product will undoubtedly reap the rewards.

9.2 Natural Language Processing for Product Interfaces

As a product manager, you're constantly seeking innovative ways to improve your products and make them more appealing to your target audience. An area that has recently gained significant popularity in enhancing product interfaces is natural language processing (NLP). In this section, we'll explore how natural language processing can help create more meaningful and seamless user experiences and discuss some key insights to navigate the complexities of NLP for product managers.

Natural language processing is a subdomain of artificial intelligence that focuses on the interaction between computers and humans through spoken and written language. The purpose of NLP is to enable computers to understand, interpret, and generate human language in a way that is both meaningful and useful to users (Hirschberg & Manning, 2015).

Before diving into how NLP can be employed for product interfaces, let's take a step back and assess an essential question: Why should we even bother with natural language processing in product management?

The answer is simple: Today's users demand more intuitive and straightforward interactions with technology. As voice-enabled assistants like Siri, Alexa, and Google Assistant continue to grow in popularity, users are becoming more accustomed to engaging with devices using natural language commands (Alonso, 2018). By integrating NLP into your product interface, you can better meet these evolving user expectations and provide more engaging experiences that set your product apart from competitors.

Now that we understand the importance of NLP in product management, let's dive into two deep insights that will help you leverage NLP in your product interfaces.

1. Keep it simple and focused.

Integrating NLP into your product can be incredibly powerful, but it's crucial to avoid overwhelming users with too many options or overcomplicated language. Research by Malmasi et al. (2018) demonstrated that simplifying text and focusing on the core message improves NLP system performance. This suggests that keeping your NLP interactions straightforward and concise will lead to better results.

As a product manager, it's essential to strike the right balance between providing a comprehensive user experience and avoiding decision paralysis. Instead of trying to incorporate every possible feature or capability in your NLP interface, focus on the most critical and widely-used user interactions. Determine the primary use cases for your target audience and emphasize the areas where natural language processing can make a significant and lasting impact.

2. Continuously learn and adapt.

Just as humans are not perfect in communicating with one another, so too are NLP systems in interpreting and producing language. Recognizing this inherent flaw is not a hindrance but an opportunity for growth. User feedback will be invaluable in refining your NLP-enriched product, and it's vital to design tools that allow continuous learning from user interactions and feedback (Agichtein et al., 2006).

Incorporate mechanisms for users to provide feedback on the accuracy and effectiveness of your NLP interface. This will help you improve the system iteratively and create an adaptive NLP system that grows and evolves with your users' needs. A feedback loop is essential, as it will make your interface more relevant, effective and market-ready, no matter how sophisticated the technology behind it is.

To sum up, incorporating natural language processing into your product interface is an impactful way to enhance the user experience and meet evolving consumer expectations. Remember to keep the interactions simple, focused, and concise and continually adapt your system using user feedback. By embracing these insights, you will be well on your way to becoming a stronger product manager who can harness the power of NLP for the benefit of your product's users.

9.3 Enhancing User Experiences with AI-Driven Features

I cannot stress enough how vital user experience (UX) is for creating successful products. A great user experience not only delights the users but also increases retention, drives organic growth, and ultimately determines the success of a product. In the rapidly changing world of technology, artificial intelligence (AI) has emerged as a frontrunner to significantly impact product management, particularly in enhancing user experiences. In this section, we will explore the various ways AI-driven features can elevate UX and discuss practical advice on how to harness these AI capabilities to create stronger products.

To begin, let us dive into the realm of AI-driven personalization. Personalization has evolved from a luxury to a necessity when it comes to user experience. In fact, according to research by Accenture (2018), 91% of consumers are more likely to shop with brands that provide relevant offers and recommendations. Employing AI capabilities to create personalized experiences allows product managers to deliver relevant content, offerings, and recommendations tailored to an individual user's preferences, behavior, and past interactions. This translates into a more satisfying and engaging experience which drives user loyalty (Jäger & Kretzberg, 2020). By harnessing rich user data and AI-driven algorithms, product managers can create effective and timely personalization, thereby significantly lifting user satisfaction.

Practical Advice:
When utilizing AI for personalization, ensure that the data collection process is transparent, and users have control over their data—anonymize or aggregate data sources as much as possible to protect user privacy. Experiment with different machine learning models to find the one that best suits your product's specific needs and customer

preferences. Lastly, always keep monitoring and improving the AI-based personalization models based on user feedback and evolving user preferences.

AI has also made significant strides in enhancing user support by introducing chatbots and virtual assistants. In fact, 61% of users claimed they would use a chatbot for help if it were available (Forbes, 2018). AI-enabled chatbots can dramatically improve users' experiences by providing fast, accurate, and personalized assistance around the clock. This, in turn, frees up resources for human customer support teams to focus on more complicated issues that require their expertise.

Deep Insight:
AI-driven customer support doesn't have to be limited to chatbots. Consider how AI can be integrated into other elements of customer support, such as automated ticket routing or sentiment analysis in customer reviews. As AI capabilities continue to improve, they could potentially identify trends or patterns in customer feedback, enabling product managers to address targeted areas of improvement.

Another AI-driven feature that can dramatically enhance UX is utilizing AI for predicting and preventing user churn. AI can analyze various factors and user behaviors within your product to identify early signs of customer dissatisfaction or reduced engagement. Armed with this information, product managers can be proactive in taking remedial action or reaching out to the user with personalized incentives, ultimately improving the user experience and reducing churn rate. By employing proactive measures such as these, you can turn potential negative user experiences into opportunities for improvement and potentially create loyal users in the long run.

Deep Insight:
User churn prediction models should be balanced optimally to avoid false alarms as well as missed opportunities. In

other words, don't let your AI model be too sensitive where it's constantly highlighting potential churn clients, but also don't allow it to be too strict where your team ends up missing users who could have benefited from a timely intervention.

In conclusion, AI-driven features hold tremendous potential to enhance user experience in numerous ways, from personalization to support and even in preventing user churn. As a product manager, it is essential to stay ahead of the curve and continually explore and experiment with incorporating AI capabilities into your product's roadmap. In doing so, you'll be creating stronger products, delivering exceptional user experiences, and ultimately achieving greater success in this competitive landscape.

9.4 The Future of AI in Product Management

The world of product management is about to be revolutionized by artificial intelligence (AI). With the rapid advancements in AI technologies, it's no wonder that product managers everywhere are excited, but also worried, about the future of their roles in the industry. This chapter will help product managers understand the incredible potential of AI for product management and provide practical advice on how it can be integrated into current and future processes.

As we venture into the unknown, it's crucial to consider emerging trends and try to anticipate how they might impact the world of product management. A recent report by McKinsey Global Institute found that by 2030, AI could add anywhere from $13 trillion to $15.8 trillion to the global economy (Chui, Manyika, and Miremadi, 2021). This growth will spillover into the product management sector in many ways, including improving operational efficiency, decision making, and overall quality of products.

Deep Insight #1: AI will augment and enhance product management skills, not replace them

It's easy to fall into the trap of thinking that AI might replace human product managers. However, instead of throwing in the towel, product managers should keep in mind that AI is a tool that can be used to enhance their skills and support their tasks, rather than supplant them (Samuel, 2018). As we've seen in other industries, AI isn't the enemy; rather, it can be a valuable ally to effectively improve decision-making and gain an edge in the market.

For instance, AI can help product managers prioritize and identify opportunities with better accuracy. By processing and analyzing vast amounts of data, AI can identify new markets, customer pain points, and potential new features for products. AI can do this far quicker than any human PM, allowing product managers to focus on crafting strategies and nurturing their existing skills.

For product managers to take full advantage of AI, they must familiarize themselves with AI tools and determine the best ways to integrate them into their existing workflows. They should be proactive in identifying opportunities to apply AI in their roles and continuously evaluate its impact on their performance.

Deep Insight #2: AI will open doors to a new era of collaboration

Another significant change AI brings to product management is the ability to improve cross-functional collaboration within organizations. As AI continues to mature and integrate into various business functions, product managers will have the opportunity to join forces with these various departments, leveraging AI insights to align goals, strengthen relations, and ultimately bring better products to market (Swaminathan, 2021).

Practical Advice: How to Embrace AI in Product Management

1. Start small and experiment: Don't aim to overhaul your entire decision-making process overnight. Instead, integrate AI into your workflow one piece at a time. Start by using AI to tackle smaller tasks or specific aspects of product development. For instance, you could use AI-powered analytics tools to analyze market trends or identify hidden customer preferences.

2. Evaluate different AI tools: Experiment with different AI tools on the market, paying close attention to their functionalities, suitability for your organization, and how well they fit within your existing workflows. Understand the potential limitations of these solutions to ensure you maintain realistic expectations.

3. Collaborate with other departments: Actively engage with other departments within your organization and explore how AI can help you work together. For instance, work with the marketing team to utilize AI in understanding consumer behaviors, targeting specific audiences, and optimizing marketing campaigns based on product features.

4. Continuously learn and adapt: The world of AI is continuously evolving; product managers should remain agile in their approach to learning about and embracing AI. Keep up with industry news and developments by attending conferences, participating in webinars, and staying informed about the latest published studies and research.

In short, the future of AI in product management is bright and full of potential. The key to success in this brave new world will be flexibility and a willingness to adapt. By viewing AI as a collaboration partner and not a competitor, product managers can harness the unparalleled power of artificial intelligence to help create groundbreaking products that delight customers and push the boundaries of what's possible.

Chapter 10: The Rise of the Product Operations Role

I have seen the field of product management evolve significantly over the last few years. One of the most essential changes in this realm has been the increasing prominence of the Product Operations role. The emergence of this role evidently highlights its significant contributions, allowing organizations to better handle their products, ensuring customer satisfaction, and increasing their bottom line. Today, we will delve deep into this emerging discipline and explore its journey, the impact it has on businesses, and how you can best integrate and optimize it in your organization. By the end of this chapter, you will have a clear understanding of Product Operations and how it can make your product management function even more powerful.

10.1 Defining Product Operations and its Importance

Product Operations is a cross-functional discipline that aims to support product management and the broader product strategy. It functions to help product teams scale, become more impactful, and operate more efficiently (Lo 2020). This role varies across different organizations; however, its main functions can typically include establishing product management best practices, collaborating with multiple departments to facilitate the development, and actively managing the life-cycle of a product.

Why has Product Operations emerged as an essential role in recent years?

First, let us consider the growth of product management as a discipline itself. As product management evolved, professionals started to specialize in various aspects, and Product Operations is no exception. Today, modern businesses offer more complex and diverse product portfolios, often necessitating dedicated support for product managers. This growing complexity gave rise to a support function that is capable of managing the increasing intricacies of product management (Valentino 2021). Thus, by establishing a dedicated Product Operations role, businesses can ensure structured support and coordination across all product teams, and streamline decision-making and execution.

Another key reason for the rise of Product Operations is the growing importance of agile and data-driven methodologies. With the swift changes in product management, companies today must rely heavily on data and information to make informed decisions about their products. Product Operations professionals have a pivotal role in data-driven decision-making, helping businesses understand their customers' needs, evaluate performance metrics, and facilitate the efficient use of resources (Lo 2020). In other words, Product Operations not only helps in streamlining product management but also empowers product teams to maintain a customer-focused, data-driven approach.

Now that we know how Product Operations emerged and its primary purposes, let's look at its impact on organizations. The Product Operations role is just as crucial as other roles in ensuring product success. Having dedicated support for your product management teams can help your organization transition from merely reactive decision-making to proactive, data-driven strategies. Furthermore, this additional support ensures a more streamlined development process and clear communication across departments.

One key insight that cannot be overlooked is that the Product Operations role should not be considered as a replacement for the product manager. Instead, it acts as a supportive enabler of product excellence, affording product management the ability to focus on strategic aspects of product development, such as devising product vision and evangelizing the importance of customer feedback (Valentino 2021). This partnership is essential for realizing the full potential of both roles.

By now, you might be intrigued and curious to know how to apply these insights and integrate Product Operations into your organization. **Here are some practical tips for embracing this function successfully:**

1. Clearly define the role of Product Operations in your organization. While the general purpose of this role remains consistent, the specific responsibilities will vary depending on your organization's size and structure. Understanding your organization's needs and goals will help you determine the appropriate level of product support required to thrive.
2. Invest in the right people. Just as hiring an exceptional product manager is essential, finding a skilled Product Operations professional is equally crucial. They need to possess excellent interpersonal and communication skills, as well as the ability to work with cross-functional teams, analyze data, and adapt to rapid changes
3. Empower Product Operations with the right resources. Invest in the tools, training, and technology that will enable your Product Operations to excel. This includes providing access to customer insights and analytics, as well as supporting their ongoing learning and development.
4. Foster collaboration between Product Operations and product teams. As mentioned earlier, these two roles should ideally function in partnership, complementing each other's efforts. Encourage open dialogue, mutual respect, and teamwork to ensure the seamless execution of your product strategy.

By implementing these practical tips and understanding the importance of this growing discipline, your organization can fully harness the power of Product Operations, enabling greater product efficiency and success.

In conclusion, the rise of the Product Operations role is a testament to the growing need for structured, data-driven support in product management. The insights mentioned above stress the importance of treating Product Operations as an essential function within your organization, and how this emergent discipline can propel product teams to achieve excellence. By recognizing and investing in the talents and skills of well-equipped Product Operations professionals, businesses have a tremendous opportunity to advance, ensuring long-term success and customer satisfaction in today's ever-evolving landscape.

10.2 Aligning Product Operations with Overall Product Strategy

Strong product managers understand that the success of their product depends on aligning all aspects of the product lifecycle with a well-formulated product strategy. In particular, product operations must be seamlessly integrated into the overall product vision to ensure maximum customer satisfaction and long-term growth. In this section, we will explore the importance of aligning product operations with your product strategy, some key considerations, and practical advice to achieve this alignment.

The Importance of Alignment

Selecting a winning product strategy is only half the battle (Anthony and Eyring, 2011). A clear, coherent plan is essential, but without the right operational infrastructure in place to support it, even the most innovative products can easily fail to reach their full potential. Aligning product operations with overall product strategy is vital for several reasons:

Efficient resource allocation. Ensuring that all resources are allocated optimally throughout the product lifecycle enables the most effective use of your budget, time, and talent.

Clear performance metrics. When your product operations are aligned with your overall product strategy, it becomes easier to measure the success of your product and to set and track relevant key performance indicators (KPIs).

Enhanced collaboration. Alignment encourages collaboration and effective communication across teams, contributing to a consistent and well-orchestrated product experience across various touchpoints.

Increased flexibility and adaptability. Alignment enables your organization to respond to external changes and capitalize on new opportunities while remaining consistent with your product strategy.

Key Considerations for Aligning Product Operations with Overall Product Strategy

Strategic Planning and Execution. Alignment begins with a robust strategic planning process that involves stakeholders across the organization (Rigby, Sutherland, and Takeuchi, 2016). As a product manager, you must work closely with key stakeholders to align goals and objectives, develop coherent roadmaps, and ensure that actions and initiatives align with your product strategy. This requires an ongoing process of review and adjustment to maintain alignment and operational effectiveness.

Process Integration. Aligning product operations with your overall product strategy involves integrating product development, go-to-market, and support activities. This can include cross-functional collaboration between teams, sharing data and insights, and aligning the efforts of different departments to create a seamless process that supports and amplifies your product strategy.

Performance Measurement. To ensure alignment, it's essential to monitor and track the performance of both your product strategy and product operations, and continually adjust to maintain alignment. Key performance indicators (KPIs) can help you measure the effectiveness of your operational activities against your strategic objectives, enabling you to identify potential problems and take corrective action as needed.

Practical Advice for Aligning Product Operations with Overall Product Strategy

Involve all stakeholders early. The worst time to try to align product operations with your product strategy is after months of development work has been completed. Instead, bring key team members from various departments together at the outset, and ensure that everyone is on the same page regarding the product strategy and the operational implications of that strategy.

Regularly review and adjust. Just as your product strategy must evolve in response to changing market conditions or customer needs, your product operations must be similarly agile. Schedule regular reviews to assess the alignment of your product operations with your overall product strategy, and make adjustments as necessary to keep things on track.

Invest in tools and technologies. Utilizing the right tools and technologies can significantly improve the efficiency and effectiveness of your product operations, ultimately helping to align them with your overarching strategy. Consider investing in specialized software to streamline processes, track performance, and promote collaboration across teams.

Be open to feedback. Your product strategy and operations alignment should be a collaborative effort, and every team member must feel comfortable providing feedback on potential misalignments or inefficiencies. Encouraging open and honest communication, and being willing to implement changes based on team input, will enhance the overall performance of your product operations and contribute to better alignment with your overall product strategy.

Deep Insights

Alignment is a continuous process. Ensuring that your product operations are aligned with overall product strategy is not a one-time exercise. Products, markets, and competitive landscapes are constantly evolving, and an alignment in place today may become disrupted tomorrow. As a product manager, you must maintain a constant focus on alignment and be willing to adjust both your product strategy and product operations in response to new information and insights.

Context is key. Achieving alignment between product operations and product strategy is crucial for overall success, but it's not a one-size-fits-all endeavor. Your product operations must be tailored to the specific context of your product, industry, organization, and customer base. Understanding your unique context, and implementing best practices accordingly, will ensure that your product operations are aligned with your overall product strategy and maximally effective in supporting your product's success.

In conclusion, aligning product operations with your overall product strategy is essential for the efficient use of resources, clear performance metrics, enhanced collaboration, and adaptability within your product management role. By focusing on strategic planning and execution, process integration, and performance measurement, and following the practical advice provided above, you can take the necessary steps to ensure that your product operations are well-aligned with your overall product strategy, ultimately boosting the performance and success of your product.

10.3 Key Responsibilities and Skills of Product Operations Managers

As we delve further into the world of product management, it's essential to explore the critical role of product operations managers. These individuals are the unsung heroes working behind the scenes to ensure that the product management process runs smoothly and efficiently. I've seen firsthand the immense value that effective product operations managers bring to the organization. So let's discuss their key responsibilities and the skills they must possess to excel in this role.

Product operations managers are responsible for tracking the effectiveness of product management processes, facilitating collaboration between various teams, and offering strategic guidance to improve the product's performance. They are the glue that holds everything together, working closely with product managers, engineers, designers, data analysts, and other stakeholders to ensure that the product is being developed, launched, and maintained efficiently and effectively (Woonyoung, 2019).

As highlighted in a study by Schuh et al. (2020), there are several crucial responsibilities and requisite skills for product operations managers. Let's take a closer look at these aspects and offer practical advice on how to enhance performance in this role.

Process Management:

Product operations managers are responsible for defining, implementing, and continuously refining product management processes. These processes may include goal-setting, roadmapping, backlog management, performance tracking, and stakeholder collaboration. A good product operations manager should be adept at identifying inefficiencies and quickly implementing improvements, ensuring that the product development process functions optimally.

Deep Insight: Become a student of best practices in product management and agile methodologies. Dedicate time to regularly reading articles, participating in webinars, and attending conferences to stay informed about the latest developments in the industry. This proactive approach will enable you to bring new and innovative process improvement ideas to your organization consistently.

Cross-Functional Collaboration:

Product ops managers must effectively collaborate with various teams within the organization, such as engineering, design, marketing, sales, and customer support. They need to build strong relationships and serve as a bridge between these teams to promote alignment, establish shared goals, and facilitate effective communication (Woonyoung, 2019).

Deep Insight: Invest in building strong, trusting relationships with team members from different functions. Take the time to understand each team's unique challenges, priorities, and contributions to the product. This understanding will enable you to facilitate better cooperation among teams and avoid potential obstacles through proactive communication.

Data-Driven Decision-Making:

Product operations managers must collect, analyze, and interpret data to identify trends, opportunities, and areas for improvement. They must be skilled in using analytical tools, generating insights from large and complex datasets, and presenting these insights in an actionable format to stakeholders. As a product operations manager, you should be able to leverage data to drive better decision-making throughout the product lifecycle.

Practical Advice: Familiarize yourself with data analytics tools and platforms relevant to your organization. Learn how to effectively visualize data and construct compelling narratives around the insights you uncover. This expertise will be invaluable in driving data-driven decision-making across the organization.

Strategic Planning:

A critical responsibility of product operations managers is to participate in the strategic planning process, working alongside product managers, leadership teams, and other stakeholders. They must understand the market trends, competitor movements, and customer feedback to offer valuable insights and help shape the product strategy (Schuh et al., 2020).

Practical Advice: Cultivate a deep understanding of your industry landscape and stay updated on relevant trends and competitive dynamics. Engage with customers and frontline teams to gather qualitative insights that complement data-driven analyses. The combination of these skills will make you a valuable contributor to the strategic planning process.

Change Management:

As organizations evolve, the role of product operations managers often involves managing change. They may be responsible for overseeing the implementation of new tools, processes, or organizational structures to support the product management function. To excel in this capacity, product ops managers must demonstrate resilience, adaptability, and strong leadership skills.

Practical Advice: Develop a change management toolkit that includes communication strategies, stakeholder mapping, and risk mitigation plans. Regularly revisit these tools and adapt your approach based on your organization's unique culture and circumstances. A thoughtful and proactive approach to change management will enable you to shepherd your organization through complex transitions with minimal disruption.

In conclusion, product operations managers play a vital role in the overall success of a product's lifecycle. By understanding and honing the key responsibilities and skills outlined above, you'll be well-equipped to contribute significantly to your organization's product management environment and ultimately, become a stronger product manager.

10.4 Integrating Product Operations into Your Team

As a product manager, you might be tempted to approach product operations as an entirely separate function or as an additional duty for a select few individuals on your team. However, to foster a truly agile and efficient working environment, it is crucial to integrate product operations fully into your entire team. Doing so will encourage your team members to understand how each person's role aligns with the overall product strategy and collaborate more effectively. In this section, we'll discuss key aspects of integrating product operations and how it can yield stronger results for your products.

Establish cross-functional collaboration

Cohen, Lindvall & Costa (2003) have recognized the importance of cross-functional teams in achieving better product performance. By encouraging collaboration between different roles, you can create a more efficient workflow, allowing team members to see the bigger picture and understand how their tasks contribute to the product's overall vision.

One way to foster cross-functional collaboration is to involve various team members in product management meetings, including data analysts, designers, engineers, and marketers. This not only allows vital information to be shared more efficiently, but it also provides an opportunity for valuable feedback and perspective from each function.

Standardize processes and procedures

A key aspect of integrating product operations into your team is having standardized processes in place. Documentation, meeting schedules, and reporting templates should be consistent and easily accessible to all team members (Daugherty, 2019).

Taking the time to create detailed documentation of workflows, decisions, product strategies, and overall objectives can help streamline future projects and ensure that everyone is on the same page. Standardized reporting templates can improve communication and simplify the tracking of progress and performance.

Encourage continuous learning and improvement

Deep Insight 1: Provide ongoing training opportunities

Investing in your team's education and development helps create a culture of continuous learning and improvement. Offering training opportunities in product management, data analysis, and other relevant areas can accelerate the integration of product operations into your team. This helps create well-rounded team members who can better understand the crucial interplay of roles and functions on the team.

Deep Insight 2: Embrace retrospectives to refine processes

Marrying product management and product operations involves ongoing refinement of processes and procedures. Regular retrospectives can provide a platform for the team to analyze their work, identify areas of improvement, and adapt accordingly. Encouraging open, honest discussions about what worked well and what didn't fosters a collaborative environment and demonstrates how operations and product management are interdependent in driving a successful product.

Utilize tools and technologies to enhance collaboration

Leveraging the right tools and technologies can improve cross-functional collaboration, data accessibility, and communication (Krisholm, 2015). Project management software, file-sharing platforms, and communication tools can facilitate team communication, track progress, and store essential product information in a central location accessible to all team members.

Emphasize the value of data-driven decisions

Fostering a data-driven culture helps your team make informed decisions that improve product performance. Incorporating data from various sources, such as user feedback, marketing analytics, and overall product usage, can enable the team to identify patterns, trends, and areas for improvement. Encouraging team members to incorporate data in their work and decision-making processes helps the team align their actions with the overall product vision and better understand the role of product operations.

In conclusion, integrating product operations into your team not only improves cross-functional collaboration but also creates an agile work environment that enables data-driven decision-making. By fostering collaboration, standardizing processes, enabling continuous learning, leveraging technology, and emphasizing the value of data, you'll create a stronger overall product management team, leading to better products and greater success in the competitive marketplace.

Chapter 11: Moving Up from Individual Contributor

Congratulations on reaching this point in your career! As a skilled individual contributor, you have excelled in your role and made considerable impact on your product or project. Now, you may be feeling a yearning for something more challenging, a sense of wanting to have more influence, the desire to inspire and lead others. Moving from an individual contributor to a product management role may be just the right step for you, and we are here to help you make that transition as smoothly as possible.

Product management is integral to the success of any organization, as it takes an idea from inception to execution and ensures that it resonates with customers. The role demands a mix of strategic thinking, technical know-how, leadership, and creative skills '96 all of which can be honed with prior experience as an individual contributor. So, take heart in knowing that you bring valuable skills to the table that can be an asset in your product management journey.

Step 1: Embrace the Challenges

The first step to successfully making the transition is to accept and be ready for the challenges that come with it. Moving into a product management role means you will be giving up the comfort of working on a single area of expertise and will instead need to become a subject-matter expert on the overall product or project. You will transition from a specialist mindset to a generalist mindset, focusing more on the big picture (Lee, 2014).

A study by CEB (now Gartner) revealed that successful product managers are quick learners who can navigate through unfamiliar situations and learn about various aspects of a business, including technology, sales, and operations (CEB Blogs, 2014). As a product manager, you will need to see the bigger picture, make consequential decisions about the product, and lead cross-functional teams. So, be prepared to embrace new challenges as you navigate this change.

Step 2: Build a Strong Network

Any position of leadership and influence requires a strong network of peers, superiors, and subordinates who can provide valuable insights and support throughout your career. A study of project managers found that those with strong social ties reported higher levels of satisfaction with their work and demonstrated better performance (Akamai, 2015). Start building your network by identifying key stakeholders, participating in relevant events or meetings, and connecting with colleagues from cross-functional teams.

A pro-active approach to networking can be a powerful way to informally talk about your aspirations, learn from others' experiences, and acquire knowledge about different aspects of a business. This, in turn, can also signal to decision-makers in your organization that you are ready and capable of taking on increased responsibility.

Step 3: Develop Key Soft Skills

One of the most distinguishing factors between individual contributors and product managers is the necessity to develop strong soft skills. While technical expertise is essential for a successful product manager, having excellent communication, negotiation, and problem-solving skills is equally important.

In a study by Miron-Spektor et al. (2011), researchers found that product managers with higher emotional intelligence (EI) were better able to manage complex business situations and bring a creative touch to their work, which led to better product innovation. Enhancing your emotional intelligence can help you build stronger relationships with your team, implement better strategies to resolve conflicts, and empower your team members to bring forth their best ideas.

Similarly, developing strong negotiation skills will enable you to align stakeholders and ensure the smooth delivery of the product. Work on refining these critical soft skills even as you master the functional aspects of product management.

Insight #1: The Power of Mentorship

Identifying a mentor can be a game-changer during your journey from individual contributor to product manager. The right mentor will provide guidance, share valuable expertise, and offer constructive feedback that can accelerate your personal and professional growth. Seek out experienced product managers who have successfully made the transition their insights will be invaluable in helping you to avoid roadblocks and to navigate new challenges.

Insight #2: Learn to Say No

One of the most important (and often difficult) skills for a product manager to master is the art of saying 'no.' As someone who is responsible for the overall vision of a product, a product manager must make strategic decisions about what features to include and which to prioritize. While it may be tempting to try to appease everyone by saying 'yes,' doing so can compromise the product's focus and ultimately dilute its impact. Learning when and how to say 'no' assertively without causing tension is crucial to maintaining the integrity of the product and success in this role.

In summary, transitioning from an individual contributor to a product management role can be a challenging yet highly rewarding experience. By embracing the challenges associated with the new role, building a broad network of peers, and strengthening your soft skills, you can set yourself up for success and achieve a lasting impact in your organization as a product manager. So, go forth, and lead with confidence, tenacity, and resilience that sets you apart as a true leader in product management.

11.1: Developing Leadership Skills and Mindset

As product managers, you are often looked upon as leaders in your organization. It is essential that you not only possess exceptional skills relevant to your domain but also have the mindset and leadership capabilities required to lead your team and products to success. As the great John Quincy Adams once said, "If your actions inspire others to dream more, learn more, do more and become more, you are a leader." And in this ever-evolving landscape of technology and business, the significance of leadership skills and mindset cannot be overstated.

In this section, we will delve into some critical aspects of leadership skills and mindset that you, as a product manager, must cultivate to achieve success and inspire others to follow suit.

Cultivate emotional intelligence

Strong leadership starts with emotional intelligence (EI), which enables you to understand and manage your own emotions and those of others. Research conducted by the Harvard Business Review demonstrates that EI involves developing four fundamental competencies: self-awareness, self-management, social awareness, and relationship management (Goleman, 1998). By honing your emotional intelligence, you can empathize and connect with your team, communicate better, reduce stress, and adapt to change.

Reflect on your emotions and thoughts: Take time to understand what triggers your emotions and how these emotions can impact your work and interactions with others.

Practice active listening: Pay close attention to what people say and respond thoughtfully. This helps build trust and strong relationships within the team.

Cultivate empathy: Put yourself in others' shoes and try to see the situation from their perspective. This will provide valuable insights to tackle challenges.

Build trust and credibility

Trust is a foundational element of leadership. According to a Forbes article on leadership essentials, the three key aspects of building trust include competence, integrity, and empathy (Dizik, 2018). When your team and stakeholders trust you, they are more likely to follow your guidance, communicate openly, and collaborate effectively.

Be transparent: Share your thought process and rationale behind decisions, as well as relevant facts and data with your team.

Consistency: Follow through on your commitments and deliver what you promise.

Show vulnerability: Admit when you don't know something or have made a mistake, this goes a long way in building credibility.

Develop a compelling product vision

As a product manager, it is crucial to create a strong, clear, and compelling product vision that guides your team and aligns with the company's strategic objectives. According to a Harvard Business Review article, having a clear vision helps motivate your team, influence stakeholders and manage the product life cycle effectively (Neeley & Garcia, 2021).

Involve your team: Encourage participation from all team members when developing the product vision to ensure everyone feels ownership and is invested in the process.

Communicate the vision effectively: Use stories and real-life examples to make the vision more relatable and understandable for your team and stakeholders.

Revisit the vision consistently: Ensure it evolves and adapts to any changes in the organization, market or customer's needs.

Empower and motivate your team

Product management is a team sport. It is, therefore, vital to motivate and inspire your team members to actively contribute to the product's success. Research published by the Journal of Applied Behavioral Science indicates that empowering leadership positively affects employees' performance by enhancing their psychological empowerment (Seibert, Wang & Courtright, 2011).

Delegate responsibilities: Provide team members with meaningful tasks and give them the autonomy to make decisions, creating a sense of ownership and investment in the project.

Encourage learning and development: Recognize each team member's strengths and weaknesses and promote continual growth by providing learning opportunities.

Recognize and reward hard work: Appreciate team members who demonstrate exceptional work, share success stories, and ensure those who contribute significantly get proper recognition.

Insight:

Balance authority and empathy: As a product manager, your role demands the ability to take decisive actions and sometimes make unpopular decisions. Simultaneously, you should be empathetic and understand the impact of these decisions on your team. Striking the right balance between authority and empathy helps you develop a strong leadership mindset and lead a high-performing team.

Adapt your leadership style: Remember that effective leadership is not a one-size-fits-all approach. Different situations and individuals may call for different leadership styles. As a product manager, it is crucial to continuously develop your leadership skills, adapt to various contexts and people, and be flexible in order to drive success in all situations.

In conclusion, developing strong leadership skills and a winning mindset takes time, effort, and conscious practice. By focusing on these essential aspects, you can strengthen your leadership prowess, foster a successful product management team, and lead your products to remarkable achievements.

11.2 Effective delegation and team empowerment

I understand that one of the critical factors in leading a highly successful product team is not only having great decision-making skills but also the ability to delegate tasks effectively and empower your team. In this section, we will delve into the two crucial aspects of honing this skill: effective delegation and team empowerment. By the end of this chapter, you'll have gained the strategies to enhance your team's performance and be well on your way to becoming a stronger product manager.

Delegation might seem like a simple concept at first glance, but it's much more than just assigning tasks to your team members. Effective delegation is about entrusting your team members with the responsibility and authority to complete certain tasks or make particular decisions on behalf of the product management team (Yukl, 2006). Learning how to delegate effectively is necessary for maximizing your team's potential and ultimately, the product's success.

Before diving into the benefits of delegation and team empowerment, let's first address a common concern that many product managers face: the fear of letting go. It's understandable that you might be hesitant to delegate, especially if you have had a hands-on approach to product management so far. However, what many product managers might fail to realize is that by holding onto tasks they should be delegating, they are hindering their team's growth and overall productivity (Kottke & K'f6rtge, 2011). A study conducted by Kottke and K'f6rtge (2011) showed that ineffective delegation of tasks led to a decrease in team motivation and overall efficiency. By relinquishing some control and giving your team room to grow, you can maximize their potential, which consequently leads to greater results for your product.

Now that we've acknowledged the importance of delegation and team empowerment, it's time to outline some best practices that will help you become a master delegator.

Identify tasks suitable for delegation: Assess your workload and determine which tasks can be delegated to your team members. This should include tasks that are time-consuming or do not strictly require your expertise (Yukl, 2006). By focusing on tasks that are crucial to the product's success and delegating others to your team members, you can make better use of your time.

Match tasks to team members skills: Effective delegation requires a good understanding of your team members strengths and weaknesses. A study conducted by Hinkin and Tracey (1999) revealed that if a task is matched to team members' skills and interests, the chances of successful delegation are significantly increased. Make sure to delegate tasks based on your team members' strengths and areas of expertise to ensure that the work is completed effectively and efficiently.

Cultivate your personal brand: Your reputation within your organization will significantly influence the success of your initiatives. Take the time to build and maintain your personal brand as a product manager. This may involve showcasing your successes, taking calculated risks to improve your visibility, and demonstrating your commitment to your organization's goals. By doing so, you will become a trusted and respected figure within your workplace, making it easier for you to garner support and sponsorship for your ideas.

Stay informed and prepared: In order to make strategically sound decisions and to mitigate potential backlashes, you must stay informed about what's happening not only on your team but also in the wider company landscape. Attend company meetings, read internal announcements, and follow the progress of other departments. This will help you discover potential allies and threats, anticipate roadblocks, and identify opportunities for your projects.

Practice diplomacy: As a product manager, you will often find yourself at the intersection of various departments and functions, which can lead to conflicts of interest and differing opinions. You must learn to manage these relationships tactfully, by actively listening to the concerns of others, resolving interpersonal conflicts, and finding common ground. Demonstrating diplomacy will help you create a positive work environment where your ideas are more likely to be well-received.

Understand and adapt to the power dynamics: Every organization has its unique power structure, consisting of formal and informal networks. Recognize the key influencers and decision-makers within your organization, and determine how they could impact your projects. Then, adjust your approach accordingly: maybe you need to engage the support of certain influencers behind the scenes, or tweak your proposal to address the concerns of key stakeholders.

delegate effectively is necessary for maximizing your team's potential and ultimately, the product's success.

Before diving into the benefits of delegation and team empowerment, let's first address a common concern that many product managers face: the fear of letting go. It's understandable that you might be hesitant to delegate, especially if you have had a hands-on approach to product management so far. However, what many product managers might fail to realize is that by holding onto tasks they should be delegating, they are hindering their team's growth and overall productivity (Kottke & K'f6rtge, 2011). A study conducted by Kottke and K'f6rtge (2011) showed that ineffective delegation of tasks led to a decrease in team motivation and overall efficiency. By relinquishing some control and giving your team room to grow, you can maximize their potential, which consequently leads to greater results for your product.

Now that we've acknowledged the importance of delegation and team empowerment, it's time to outline some best practices that will help you become a master delegator.

Identify tasks suitable for delegation: Assess your workload and determine which tasks can be delegated to your team members. This should include tasks that are time-consuming or do not strictly require your expertise (Yukl, 2006). By focusing on tasks that are crucial to the product's success and delegating others to your team members, you can make better use of your time.

Match tasks to team members skills: Effective delegation requires a good understanding of your team members strengths and weaknesses. A study conducted by Hinkin and Tracey (1999) revealed that if a task is matched to team members' skills and interests, the chances of successful delegation are significantly increased. Make sure to delegate tasks based on your team members' strengths and areas of expertise to ensure that the work is completed effectively and efficiently.

Provide clear directions and expectations: When delegating, it's essential to communicate the objectives and expectations for each task clearly. This will help your team members understand the significance of their role and how it contributes to the overall product's success. Providing ongoing feedback during the execution of the task will further help team members to better monitor their progress and make improvements when deemed necessary.

Give autonomy and encourage ownership: Team empowerment goes hand-in-hand with effective delegation. According to an article by Yun et al. (2012), employees who were empowered exhibited high levels of motivation, job satisfaction, and overall productivity. Empowering your team means giving them the autonomy to make decisions, solve problems, and take ownership of their work. Maintaining an open-door policy that encourages team members to share their ideas and express their concerns can contribute significantly to fostering an empowered environment.

Foster a culture of trust and support: One of the deep insights to effective delegation and team empowerment is building trust within your team. Trust and open communication can alleviate any fears of delegating tasks and empower your team members to perform at their best. Make a conscious effort to trust your team's abilities and show your support by being available to provide assistance when required.

In conclusion, the ability to delegate tasks effectively and empower your team is essential in the pursuit of becoming a stronger product manager. Keep these practices in mind as you begin delegating tasks and nurturing an empowered environment within your product team. By doing so, you'll not only foster a healthy work culture but also build a resilient team well-equipped to face the many challenges that product development may bring. Remember, your team's success is your success, and the ultimate success of your product relies on taking the time to invest in effective delegation and team empowerment strategies.

11.3 Navigating Organizational Politics

As a product manager, you will inevitably face organizational politics in your journey to becoming a stronger product leader. Organizational politics are the informal, unofficial, and often behind-the-scenes efforts by individuals and groups to gain influence, status, power, or resources within a workplace (Motta, Cuntigh, & Errichiello, 2019). This is not intrinsically negative, and in some cases, it can even be beneficial to your career if you develop the ability to navigate these political waters effectively. In this section, we will explore ways to better understand the political landscape of your organization and how you can use that knowledge to advance your ideas and projects.

First, let's acknowledge that organizational politics are not going away. In fact, according to a study by Sointu, Elovainio, and Linna (2009), the perception of organizational politics among employees is directly related to job stress and job satisfaction. This means that understanding and managing these political dynamics should be integral to your role as a product manager. So, let's delve into some practical advice for navigating these inevitable political waters.

Build your network: Developing an extensive network of relationships within your organization is crucial to understanding its political atmosphere. Engage both your colleagues in the product management sphere and those in other departments, like sales, marketing, and development. This will help you better understand their goals, motivations, and potential support for or opposition to your initiatives. Furthermore, networking allows you to identify key players and decision-makers, giving you insight into who you can turn to for support when challenges arise.

Cultivate your personal brand: Your reputation within your organization will significantly influence the success of your initiatives. Take the time to build and maintain your personal brand as a product manager. This may involve showcasing your successes, taking calculated risks to improve your visibility, and demonstrating your commitment to your organization's goals. By doing so, you will become a trusted and respected figure within your workplace, making it easier for you to garner support and sponsorship for your ideas.

Stay informed and prepared: In order to make strategically sound decisions and to mitigate potential backlashes, you must stay informed about what's happening not only on your team but also in the wider company landscape. Attend company meetings, read internal announcements, and follow the progress of other departments. This will help you discover potential allies and threats, anticipate roadblocks, and identify opportunities for your projects.

Practice diplomacy: As a product manager, you will often find yourself at the intersection of various departments and functions, which can lead to conflicts of interest and differing opinions. You must learn to manage these relationships tactfully, by actively listening to the concerns of others, resolving interpersonal conflicts, and finding common ground. Demonstrating diplomacy will help you create a positive work environment where your ideas are more likely to be well-received.

Understand and adapt to the power dynamics: Every organization has its unique power structure, consisting of formal and informal networks. Recognize the key influencers and decision-makers within your organization, and determine how they could impact your projects. Then, adjust your approach accordingly: maybe you need to engage the support of certain influencers behind the scenes, or tweak your proposal to address the concerns of key stakeholders.

Play the long game: Navigating organizational politics effectively means playing the long game. Be patient, strategic, and persistent in your pursuit of your goals, understanding that progress may be slow at times. Be willing to compromise when it's advantageous, but also hold firm to your convictions when it's essential to do so.

What to consider when navigating organizational politics are:

Personal power trumps positional power: According to Pfeffer (2010), personal influence and competence are more critical for success in organizations than formal authority or title. To navigate organizational politics effectively, you should focus on developing your personal power '96 your expertise, relationships, and communication skills '96rather than relying solely on your job title.

Organizational politics can benefit your growth: While organizational politics are often viewed negatively, they can provide valuable opportunities for personal and professional growth. By engaging in political activities ethically and effectively, you can enhance your visibility, improve your relationships with stakeholders, and increase your influence within your organization (Motta et al., 2019). This can lead to a more fulfilling and successful career in product management.

In conclusion, navigating organizational politics is a crucial aspect of becoming a stronger product manager. Cultivate a strategic mindset and resilience, as you work to understand and influence the political landscape within your organization. Your ability to skilfully manoeuvre these waters will determine how effectively you can promote and implement your ideas, and ultimately, steer your career towards success.

I cannot stress enough the importance of building a strong personal brand that sets you apart from the competition in the world of product leadership. The reason being, product management is an ever-evolving field that requires professionals to adapt fast and be quick thinkers. A strong personal brand allows you to showcase your unique perspective, strategy-driven mindset, and innovative approach to problem-solving. This chapter will discuss the essential steps to building your personal brand as a product leader and explore some research-backed strategies for standing apart in the dog-eat-dog world of product innovation.

Before getting into the nitty-gritty, it's essential to understand what personal branding is and why it's so relevant to product management. A personal brand doesn't just mean having an impressive LinkedIn profile or a well-written CV. According to Ranzetta and Kucherov (2016), personal branding refers to the practice of "managing image and reputation across multiple platforms to create personal differentiation and competitive advantage." In other words, your personal brand is your unique value proposition to the world and the ecosystem of product management.

So, how do you build a strong personal brand as a product leader? Let's dive into some practical advice and deep insights to help you pave the way to success:

1. Develop a compelling narrative

Product leaders must have a story that reflects their professional journey, achievements, passion, and, most importantly, their unique approach to product management. According to Shevchuk, Pelau, and Chiritescu (2018), a narrative is an effective personal branding tool, as it helps leaders create emotional connections by sharing personal experiences, insights, and values. Think about what differentiates you from other product managers and focus on those aspects when telling your story.

To create an impactful narrative, you can start by answering the following questions:

- What inspired you to become a product manager?
- What significant challenges have you faced throughout your professional journey, and how did you overcome them?
- What is your unique approach to product management?
- How do you stay relevant in this ever-evolving field?

2. Establish your online presence

In the digital age, your online presence is one of the most crucial aspects of personal branding. You need to be able to show that you are a thought leader in the product management space. Start by optimizing your LinkedIn profile as recruiters and potential clients will most likely explore your profile before any engagement. Make sure to have an up-to-date and informative CV, a professional profile picture, and a catchy headline that reflects your unique value proposition as a product leader.

But don't stop at LinkedIn - take advantage of other social media platforms to showcase your expertise. Share articles, news, and opinions on the latest trends in product management, participate in relevant discussions and forums, and connect with other product leaders in your niche. Regularly publishing articles or blogs on relevant platforms, such as Medium, can also demonstrate your level of expertise (Ranzetta & Kucherov, 2016).

3. Cultivate relationships & network

Building a strong network is crucial for product managers, as it can offer access to unique opportunities and insights within the field, strengthen credibility, and help you get noticed by potential clients/employers. Attend events, webinars, and conferences to expand your professional network actively. Also, remember that branding is not just about self-promotion; it's about connecting with others and sharing diverse perspectives. Be open to learning from other professionals in the field and actively contribute to the growth and development of product management as a whole community.

Deep Insight #1: Be a perpetual student

In a field where trends shift rapidly and consumer preferences evolve every other day, product leaders must invest in their continuous learning journey. By regularly updating your skills and staying current with the latest methodologies, tools, and innovations, you display your passion towards the profession and demonstrate your adaptability to change. As a result, you become more competent and attractive to potential employers, clients, and peers - this will further reinforce your personal brand as a top product leader.

Deep Insight #2: Give back to the community

Sharing your knowledge, expertise, and time with the product management community is an excellent way to solidify your brand image. You can do this by speaking at events, offering workshops, or holding informal get-togethers for like-minded individuals. This not only showcases your commitment to the growth of the product management field but also allows you to build and maintain a reputation as a respected figure within the community. Contribute to forums, offer mentorship opportunities, or even create educational content (like articles, videos, or podcasts). These activities can also contribute to your personal brand as a product leader who is dedicated and passionate about the field.

By following the advice and insights shared in this section, you can carve out a strong personal brand that highlights your exceptional capabilities as a product leader. Remember, consistency is key. Just like building any brand, building your personal brand takes time, effort, and dedication - but the payoff is worth it when you find yourself standing apart in the ever-challenging world of product management.

Chapter 12: New Idea Generation and Innovation

If you're a part of the product development world, then you already know how vital new ideas are to the success and longevity of a business. For product managers, driving innovation comes with the territory since it's their primary goal to identify and develop products that will provide significant value to customers. In this chapter, we'll explore some key strategies for new idea generation and how to foster an environment of innovation within your company.

Unlocking Creativity Through External Sources

While it is possible to source new ideas internally, looking outward can sometimes bring in a wealth of knowledge and fresh perspectives. It's important not to limit yourself when it comes to seeking external inspiration. Here are a few ways you can tap into external sources:

Mine social media and online forums: Websites like Reddit, Quora, and LinkedIn are gold mines for unearthing fresh ideas, as users often discuss pain points and potential solutions related to specific industries or markets (Acar & van den Ende, 2016). By monitoring these platforms, you can stay informed about customer and market developments.

Follow industry influencers: Industry influencers often share thought-provoking content, such as opinions, trends, and future predictions. Following them on social media platforms or subscribing to their blogs/newsletters can help you stay ahead of the curve.

Attend networking events and conferences: Attending events and conferences within your industry can expose you to new perspectives, case studies, and innovative approaches, which can lead to fresh ideas.

Collaborate with other organizations: Sometimes the best source of innovation comes from collaborating with external organizations that have complementary strengths (Enkel et al., 2009). This can range from attending hackathons to partnering with startups on joint projects.

Fostering a Culture of Innovation

Effective innovation begins with a company culture that encourages experimentation, taking risks, and learning from failures. Here are two deep insights into fostering a culture of innovation and encouraging continuous idea generation:

Innovation can't be mandated from the top down it has to be encouraged, fostered, and supported. This starts by empowering employees to contribute their ideas and giving them a sense of ownership over the process. Ensure there is a clear channel for communicating and celebrating ideas, regardless of their origin, and that every team member has the chance to contribute.

Additionally, many employees will only take the risk of sharing their ideas if they feel like it's a safe space to do so. This means embracing failures as learning opportunities, and providing time and resources for experimentation (Edmondson, 2018).

Structured collaboration and cross-functional teams.

Another way to foster innovation is through structured collaboration sessions, where different teams come together to exchange ideas and tackle challenges. Cross-functional collaboration not only provides new perspectives but also leads to stronger ideas and potential solutions.

For instance, design thinking workshops, where employees have the chance to work through various challenges in a structured and guided way, can lead to better idea generation and collaboration. By incorporating cross-functional teams into ideation sessions, you'll bring various perspectives and experiences into the room, increasing the likelihood of impactful innovation.

Practical Tips

While the above insights provide a good overview, here are some practical tips to keep in mind as you drive new idea generation and innovation:

Make time for brainstorming sessions: Schedule regular brainstorming sessions with your team to encourage free-flowing ideas. One popular technique is the "brainwriting" method, where team members take turns writing down their ideas and building upon others' contributions.

Encourage diversity of thought: Teams with a diversity of backgrounds, disciplines, and perspectives are more likely to generate creative ideas. Encourage diversity within your team and foster an environment that embraces different perspectives.

Keep customer needs at the forefront: Innovation should always be tied back to customer needs. Make sure your team understands your target customers, their pain points, and motivations. This will help generate ideas that address real customer problems.

Practice iterative development: Instead of trying to create the perfect product from the get-go, embrace the idea of building a Minimum Viable Product (MVP) and iterating based on customer feedback. This iterative process can lead to more innovation and better overall products.

New idea generation and innovation are essential components of successful product management. By embracing external sources of inspiration, fostering a culture of innovation, and employing practical tips, you'll be well on your way to developing products that stand out among the competition and resonate with your customers. Remember to continuously iterate, learn from failures, and always be open to new ideas your customers and your company will be better for it.

12.1 Cultivating a Culture of Innovation

When it comes to innovation, one of the key factors in determining a company's success is not just the quality of the ideas themselves, but the culture within the organization. A strong, innovative culture allows for ideas to be created, shared, and executed smoothly and efficiently. This, in turn, leads to better products and stronger customer relationships (Gupta, 2019). In this chapter, we will explore the crucial elements of cultivating a culture of innovation and discuss practical ways product managers can foster an innovative atmosphere within their teams and organizations.

"Innovation distinguishes between a leader and a follower." - Steve Jobs

Understanding Innovation Culture

At its core, an innovation culture nurtures and encourages the generation and implementation of fresh ideas. It revolves around the belief that every individual has the potential to contribute innovative ideas, the organization places a premium on creative thinking and problem-solving abilities, and that progress can come from both successes and failures (Lee & Trimi, 2020). By cultivating an innovation culture, product managers can significantly increase the chances of identifying breakthrough opportunities and enhance the overall product development process.

Here are some fundamental elements of an innovation culture:

1. Continuous Improvement: A commitment to consistently improving products, processes, and ways of working.
2. Open Communication: Encouraging open and honest dialogue among team members, which fosters greater collaboration and better ideas.
3. Autonomy: Allowing team members to have a say in how they accomplish their work, which can lead to new and improved ways of doing things.
4. Risk-Taking: Embracing intelligent risk-taking and learning from failures, thereby promoting an entrepreneurial mindset.
5. Harnessing Diversity: Recognizing that diverse ideas and perspectives are critical to discovering unique solutions to problems.

How Product Managers Can Foster Innovation

To create and sustain an innovative culture, product managers need to lead their teams and organizations by example. Here are some specific ways you can foster innovation as a product manager:

Emphasize the importance of problem-solving: Encourage your team to think critically and creatively about the challenges they face, focusing on understanding the root causes and developing novel solutions. By emphasizing problem-solving rather than just focusing on capabilities, you help foster a mindset where innovation is valued.

Create a safe space for idea generation: Do not dismiss any idea without first discussing and analyzing its merits. Foster an environment where all ideas are welcome and everyone's contribution is valued, regardless of their title or experience (Hoena, 2017). Routinely hold brainstorming sessions where team members are encouraged to think outside the box, and ensure all contributions are acknowledged and appreciated.

Nurture learning and experimentation: Provide opportunities for team members to learn and experiment with new technologies and methodologies. Encourage them to attend conferences, participate in workshops, and collaborate with other teams within the organization. This promotes cross-pollination of ideas and strengthens the overall innovation culture.

Develop a systematic innovation process: A structured approach to idea generation and implementation helps ensure that innovative ideas get the attention and resources they need to succeed (Lee & Trimi, 2020). Develop an innovation pipeline, with clearly defined stages and checkpoints that guide ideas from conception through to implementation. This approach not only empowers team members by giving them ownership of their ideas but also ensures the best ideas are pursued and implemented.

Collaborate with external partners: Seek input and collaboration from external partners, such as suppliers, customers, and competitors. These partnerships can provide fresh perspectives and insights, ultimately fueling the innovation process. Knowledge sharing and open collaboration is the bedrock of a vibrant innovation culture.

Recognize and reward innovation: Create a system that rewards innovative efforts, even if they don't always lead to immediate success. Recognition can be as simple as a mention in a team meeting or as formal as an award or bonus, but the important thing is to consistently recognize and celebrate innovative thinking and accomplishments.

In conclusion, cultivating a culture of innovation is not only central to the success of product managers, but it's integral to the growth and development of your entire organization. By fostering an environment where ideas are encouraged, valued, and rewarded, product managers can play an essential role in leading their teams and companies toward sustained success and growth.

12.2 Design thinking and creative problem-solving

I can assert that successful product managers are not just strategists and organizers; they are also creative thinkers who excel in designing innovative solutions to complex problems. In this section, we will explore design thinking and creative problem-solving techniques that you can use to become a stronger and more effective product manager. By the end of this section, you will have a deeper understanding of the power of design thinking and how to integrate it into your product management toolkit.

Design thinking is a human-centered, iterative approach to solving problems and creating innovative solutions by empathizing with users, defining the problem, ideating solution options, prototyping, and testing (Brown, 2008). It has gained significant traction in recent years, with many companies and organizations adopting this approach to drive innovation, foster greater creativity, and better meet the needs of their customers or users.

Research supports the value of design thinking as a means to improve product development outcomes, team collaboration, and customer satisfaction. An HBR study suggests that companies implementing design thinking and dedicating resources to it have outperformed those following a traditional approach in terms of revenue and shareholder returns (Liedtka & Ogilvie, 2011). Therefore, incorporating design thinking into your product management process can be a game-changer.

So, let's dive deeper into the design thinking process and discover practical advice to integrate it into your product management process.

Empathize:

This is the first step of design thinking, and it is where you need to understand the needs, motivations, and aspirations of your target audience. This involves conducting user research, observing users in their environment, conducting interviews, and creating user personas. By putting yourself in the shoes of your users, you can better understand their pain points and create products that truly cater to their needs.

Deep Insight: Empathy not only helps in understanding user problems but also in building an emotional connection with the users. By truly understanding their emotions and thoughts, you can develop products that create a long-lasting bond between the users and the product.

Define:

In this stage, synthesizing your research findings and clearly defining the problem you want to solve is crucial. It helps your team stay focused on the user's needs and narrows down the scope of potential solutions. Once the problem is clearly defined, make sure there is alignment across the team members.

Practical advice: When defining the problem, strive to make it specific, actionable, and user-centric. This ensures that your team stays focused on the right problem and does not get lost in generalizations or vague descriptions.

Ideate:

The ideation stage is your opportunity to challenge the status quo and explore a wide range of diverse solutions to the problem you defined. Encourage your team to engage in brainstorming sessions, World Caf'e9, mind-mapping, or SCAMPER (Substitute, Combine, Adapt, Modify, Put to another use, Eliminate, Reverse) to generate as many ideas as possible.

Deep Insight: During ideation, encourage an environment with no judgments '97 every idea counts! A culture of creative openness can lead to unique insights and unexpected connections between seemingly unrelated ideas.

Prototype:

In this stage, develop a working prototype or model of your solution to test its viability, gather feedback, and identify areas for improvement. It doesn't have to be a high-fidelity prototype; simple sketches, mock-ups, or even role-plays can work depending on the product you are designing.

Practical advice: Remember that prototyping is a way to learn and iterate quickly. Start with simple, low-cost materials that enable you to visualize your solution, gather feedback, and iterate on your design effectively.

Test:

Test your prototype with actual users to collect data and insights that validate or negate your solution assumptions. Observe users interacting with the prototype, ask questions about their experience, and take notes on their feedback. Use this feedback to iterate on your design and refine your solution.

Practical advice: When testing your prototype, be open to criticism and be prepared to iterate on your design. Embrace failures and learn from them '97 they will make your product stronger.

Design thinking emphasizes the importance of constant iteration, learning from your users, and adapting your solutions to meet their needs. As a product manager, incorporating design thinking into your work process can lead to more creative, user-centric, and effective product development outcomes.

Remember, the goal is not to follow design thinking as a rigid process but to use its principles to guide your thinking and decision-making while you work with your team to develop innovative, user-centric products.

To conclude, be an empathetic listener, have a growth mindset, and foster a culture of open-mindedness and collaboration within your organization. Nurturing your creative problem-solving skills and embracing design thinking can make you a stronger and more effective product manager.

12.3 Harnessing the Power of Brainstorming and Ideation Techniques

As a product manager, one of the critical skills you'll need to master is the art of brainstorming and ideation. Some of the greatest products emerged from inventive brainstorming sessions that steered groups of individuals to dream, imagine, and push the boundaries of what's possible (Isaksen, Dorval, & Treffinger, 2011). As an expert in product management, I am a firm believer in the power of these techniques, and in this section, I will guide you through how to effectively harness this power to become a stronger product manager.

Brainstorming, in essence, is the process of generating new ideas and solutions, usually through a group-driven, free-flowing exchange of thoughts. It is built upon the premise that when we remove our constraints and share openly, we are bound to generate a myriad of ideas from which innovative solutions can arise. Design thinking is the epitome of this process, as it provides a framework for understanding empathy, defining problems, and brainstorming innovative solutions.

Insight 1: Create an open and diverse environment

One of the key ingredients for successful brainstorming is creating an environment that encourages open, uninhibited, and diverse contributions from all participants. According to a study by Dugosh, Paulus, Roland, and Yang (2000), the best ideation and brainstorming sessions take place in an atmosphere where everyone feels comfortable to candidly share ideas, regardless of how wild or unconventional they are. Encouraging diverse perspectives and creating a judgement-free zone ensures that participants bring a wealth of unique experience, knowledge, and insights to the table, resulting in more original and refined ideas.

Practical advice: Set some ground rules before the brainstorming session to ensure all participants feel supported and respected. Emphasize that there are no 'bad' ideas and encourage everyone to contribute. Additionally, inviting people from different backgrounds and disciplines can be very effective in sourcing a wider range of ideas.

Insight 2: Leverage various ideation techniques

Another essential piece of the puzzle is utilizing various brainstorming and ideation techniques to maximize your ideation process. Research suggests that tweaking the classic brainstorming approach '96 such as incorporating certain structured techniques '96 can significantly enhance idea generation (Kohn & Smith, 2011). Techniques like mind mapping, brainwriting, or the nominal group technique can help participants visualize their thoughts more effectively and stimulate associations between seemingly unrelated concepts.

Practical Techniques

Mind mapping: Begin with a central concept, then draw branches to related sub-concepts. This helps visualize relationships between ideas and encourages new perspectives.

Brainwriting: Instead of verbally discussing ideas, each participant writes down as many ideas as possible on index cards or post-it notes for a predetermined time. They then pass their ideas to the next person, who can build upon or modify them. This assists in preventing loud voices from dominating the session and facilitates more equal contributions.

Nominal group technique: Each team member silently writes down their ideas, then team members take turns sharing them one-by-one. After discussing and refining the ideas, participants use a structured voting process to prioritize the most promising ones. This engages everyone in the ideation process and guards against groupthink.

Remember that your role as a product manager is to facilitate the ideation process, and the best way to do that is to employ a structured, well-organized approach that empowers participation and creativity.

To become a stronger product manager, embrace the power of brainstorming and ideation techniques as part of your toolkit. The effectiveness of these techniques relies on a combination of creating an open, diverse environment and employing a range of ideation strategies that suit the unique needs and goals of your team. Tune into the creative energy that emerges from these sessions, channel it into your work, and you'll no doubt witness the birth of some truly groundbreaking products.

12.4 Evaluating and Selecting the Best Ideas for Execution

Welcome to another important section in your journey towards becoming a stronger product manager. I have experienced the challenges and rewards of evaluating and selecting the best ideas for project execution. In this section, we will explore essential techniques, learn from research studies, and discover deep insights that will enable you to evaluate and select the best ideas effectively.

Why is evaluation and selection crucial?

No matter how skilled you are at generating ideas, not all of them will be good or viable. The ability to evaluate and select the best ideas is crucial for your success as a product manager. Choosing the right ideas can lead to successful product launches, increased market share, and stronger brand reputation. On the other hand, choosing the wrong ideas can result in wasted resources, time, and potentially damaging the company's reputation.

Strategies for evaluating and selecting the best ideas

When identifying the best ideas for execution, follow these strategies:

Establish clear evaluation criteria: Prioritize criteria that directly align with your organization's strategic objectives (Cooper & Edgett, 2008). Some possible criteria to consider include:

- Market potential
- Competitive advantage
- Financial feasibility

☐ Technical feasibility

Filter out ideas that dont meet your minimum threshold:
These are ideas that clearly don't align with your goals or don't
meet the minimum requirements.

Engage stakeholders: Involve stakeholders in the idea
evaluation process. Not only does this help ensure you are
considering perspectives from different functions and levels in
the organization, but it can also improve buy-in and
commitment when it time to execute the selected ideas
(Brown & Anthony, 2011).

Iterate and refine: Ideas may require several iterations before
they are ready for execution. Be open to modifying, refining, or
combining ideas based on feedback and evolving
circumstances.

Applying research findings to your evaluation process

A research study conducted by Cooper, Edgett, and
Kleinschmidt (2001) reveals that the quality of the idea-
generation process can have a significant impact on the success
of a new product project. The study found that companies that
invested in effective idea generation and evaluation techniques
experienced a 200% improvement in new product
performance.

To integrate these findings into your evaluation and selection
process:

☐ Ensure your idea generation process encourages
diverse perspectives and input from various sources.
☐ Be diligent in capturing and recording ideas for future
evaluation.
☐ Develop a consistent, transparent, and rigorous
evaluation process.
☐ Continually improve your idea evaluation process
through feedback and learning from past experiences.

How to inform your idea evaluation and selection

Deep Insight #1: Remember that the goal is not to find "the one" perfect idea but to select a combination of ideas that collectively move your product or portfolio forward. Don'92t be afraid to break down big ideas into smaller components that can be implemented sequentially or concurrently.

Deep Insight #2: Be willing to let go of ideas that, although initially promising, do not withstand the evaluation process. Don't allow sunk costs or personal attachment to prevent you from abandoning an idea when it becomes clear that it'92s not the right fit or the right time.

By applying these strategies and insights, you can become more confident in your ability to evaluate and select the best ideas for execution. With practice, you will find that your decision-making improves, your organization benefits from better product launches, and you continue to grow as a stronger product manager.

Chapter 13: Research-Driven Insights and Future Trends

As a product manager, your ultimate goal is to create products that will solve people's problems, delight them, and have a meaningful impact on their lives. This can only be achieved if you, as a product manager, dig deep into the current state of your industry and keep an eye on the future trends.

One key area of focus for successful product managers is using well-honed research and data-driven insights to guide their decisions. In this section, we'll delve into the importance of research-driven insights, explore some future trends in product management, and discover how you can apply these findings to your career.

The Importance of Research-Driven Insights

Effective product managers are data-driven decision-makers. By using research-driven insights, you can make more informed judgments, minimize the risks associated with your decisions, and create stronger, more successful products. In today's fast-paced environment, companies that adopt data-driven approaches are more likely to find success than those that rely solely on intuition and judgment (Marr, 2017).

A study conducted by McKinsey Global Institute found that companies that incorporate data analysis to support decision-making increase their chances of finding profitable growth opportunities by 23 times and are 19 times more likely to achieve above-average profitability (McKinsey, 2011). Indeed, these numbers alone emphasize the importance of research-driven insights in product management.

Integrating Research-Driven Insights into Your Product Strategy

Incorporating research-driven insights into your product strategy may seem daunting; however, it involves a few simple steps.

1. Identify the key research areas: The first step is to identify the key research areas relevant to your product. These areas might include market analysis, competitor benchmarking, understanding customer needs, and monitoring future trends.
2. Gather data: Obtain relevant and reliable data through various channels, such as customer interviews, surveys, and analytics tools.
3. Analyze the data: Once you have the data, analyze it to extract actionable insights that can be applied to your product strategy.
4. Apply insights: Take the findings from your research and analytics, and apply them to your product decisions.

Example: Imagine that your research shows a significant number of your customers are accessing your app via mobile devices. It may be worth focusing on optimizing your mobile app experience or developing new mobile-specific features that cater to your users' needs.

Embracing Future Trends in Product Management

Now that you understand the value of research-driven insights, it's equally important to keep an eye on future trends that could shape the product management landscape.

Focus on Agile Methodologies: With the rapidly changing technology landscape, product managers increasingly adopt agile methodologies that embrace change and allow for rapid iteration. Implementing agile methodologies and using data-driven insights to iterate and improve your product will be essential to staying competitive (Cohen, 2020).

Increasing Role of AI and Machine Learning: Artificial Intelligence (AI) and machine learning are increasingly being adopted by organizations to make more informed decisions and to automate complex and repetitive tasks. As a product manager, you need to stay up to date with advancements in these areas and incorporate them into your product strategy wherever relevant.

Deep Insights

Now that we've explored the importance of research-driven insights and examined the future trends in product management, let's dive into two deep insights you can apply in your career:

Balance between quantitative and qualitative research: Integrate both quantitative and qualitative research methods to paint a complete picture of your customer needs and preferences. Quantitative research provides the numerical data needed to make informed decisions, while qualitative research helps understand the underlying reasons driving customer behavior (Rice, 2019). As a product manager, you need to strike the right balance between these research methods to gain a holistic understanding and make better decisions.

Example: If your research shows that customers are spending more time on a specific page of your app but are not converting, conduct customer interviews or focus groups to understand the reasons behind this behavior and identify any barriers to conversion.

Adopt a data-driven culture: Instill a data-driven culture within your team, encouraging every team member to make data-informed decisions. By doing so, you empower individuals to contribute effectively to product decisions, and also help them justify their choices to other stakeholders.

Remember, research-driven insights are not just about gathering data; it's about analyzing that data and turning it into knowledge, understanding, and actionable insights for your product roadmap. By staying attuned to future trends and integrating research into your product strategy, you set yourself on the path to becoming a stronger product manager.

13.1 Applying Behavioral Science to Product Design

As product managers, it's essential not just to design a great product but also to understand how users will interact with it being able to predict and shape their behavior is a crucial step toward meeting customer needs more effectively. In this chapter, we will explore how behavioral science can help you optimize your product design in a way that resonates with your users and encourages the desired outcomes.

Behavioral science is the interdisciplinary study of how contextual factors and cognitive processes influence our decision-making, emotions, and actions. It's become increasingly popular in product management circles thanks to the work of researchers like Daniel Kahneman and Richard Thaler, who found entirely new ways to explain and predict human behavior through their respective books, Thinking, Fast and Slow (2011), and Nudge (2008).

Developing a good understanding of behavioral science can help you create more intuitive, engaging, and persuasive products. So, let's dive into how to apply behavioral science to your product design by examining a few key principles and examples.

Understanding Cognitive Biases

Cognitive biases are systematic errors in our thinking and decision-making process that often lead to irrational choices. As a product manager, it's essential to be aware of these biases so that you can counteract their negative effects and shape user behavior in a more predictable manner.

For instance, the "endowment effect" is a bias where people tend to overvalue things they already own compared to those they don't (Kahneman, Knetsch & Thaler, 1990). By incorporating features that make users more attached to your product, such as personalization, early investment, or progress tracking, you can help increase their perceived value of your product and boost engagement, retention, or even willingness to pay.

Another common cognitive bias is the "anchoring effect," where people tend to rely heavily on the first piece of information they encounter when making decisions (Tversky & Kahneman, 1974). This can be used to shape user behavior by strategically presenting information or pricing options, helping users make choices that are in line with your business goals.

Leveraging Social Influence

Social influence is another powerful force that drives user behavior. Cialdini (2007) has identified six principles of persuasion that you can integrate into your product design to shape users' actions: reciprocity, commitment and consistency, social proof, authority, liking, and scarcity.

For instance, implementing social proof such as user reviews, testimonials, or "most popular" tags can help new users feel more confident in trying your product or adopting specific features. The principle of scarcity can be applied by offering limited-time promotions, exclusive content, or limited access, which can create a sense of urgency and encourage users to take the desired action.

Designing for Habit Formation

Designing your product to facilitate habit formation is another way to harness the power of behavioral science. This involves understanding the "hook model" developed by Nir Eyal (2014), which consists of four stages: trigger, action, reward, and investment.

Triggers can be external (like a notification) or internal (a user feeling bored), which leads to the action stage. The action should be simple and easy to perform so that users can quickly experience the reward, like a sense of accomplishment, new content, or social validation. Finally, the investment stage can be users adding personal content or building a history of use, making them more likely to return and use the product again.

To incorporate the hook model in your product design, you need first to identify the triggers and actions that are integral to your users' experience. Next, consider how you can offer immediate and satisfying rewards after the action, and finally, think about ways to encourage users to invest in your product, helping them build a routine and fostering long-term engagement.

Key Takeaways

Behavioral science offers valuable insights into human psychology that every product manager should consider when designing products. Here are two key takeaways from this section:

Be aware of cognitive biases and use them to create more persuasive product designs. Understanding how users make decisions and which factors may sway them can help you create products that resonate with their needs and align with your business goals.

Design products that facilitate habit formation and social influence. By leveraging principles like social proof, scarcity, and the hook model, you can create more engaging products that keep users coming back for more.

By understanding and applying these behavioral science principles, you can create products that are not only useful and delightful but also better aligned with your users' mindsets, preferences, and long-term success. So don't be afraid to dig deep into the world of behavioral science and unleash its potential to enhance your product design skills.

13.2 Neuromarketing and Emotional Triggers

As a product manager, you probably already understand that the key to the success of your product lies in understanding your customers and their needs. Your role in optimizing your product involves not only understanding the functional aspects that your customers care about but also delving into their psychology to understand their emotional needs. In this section, we will dive into the world of neuromarketing and explore how you can use emotional triggers to improve the appeal and success of your product.

Neuromarketing is an interdisciplinary field that combines neuroscience and marketing to better understand how humans respond to marketing stimuli (Morrin & Ratneshwar, 2003). The aim is to gain insights into the customer's subconscious mind and create a more effective communication strategy, eventually influencing their purchasing decisions. An awareness of neuromarketing techniques can be a valuable addition to your skillset as a product manager, given the potential to develop more hypnotic messaging and stronger emotional connections with your customers.

To begin unraveling the complex world of neuromarketing and emotional triggers, let's first explore the two dominant emotional systems in our brain: the approach and the avoidance system. These systems work as two guiding forces, shaping and biasing our choices and actions around distinct goals (Elliot, 2008). It's essential to understand how these systems establish preferences and how to use them to create compelling messages for your product.

The approach system is driven by positive emotions and seeks rewards and pleasant experiences. When this system is activated, it drives us towards things that we perceive as desirable, like good food, enjoyable experiences, and social connections. On the other hand, the avoidance system, governed by negative emotions, strives to protect us from harm and to avoid potential dangers. Each of these systems operates based on different emotional triggers, leading to different decision-making processes.

It's worth mentioning that emotions play a significant role in our everyday decision-making, including purchasing decisions. For instance, researchers found that emotional responses to advertisements were more reliable predictors of purchasing behaviors than self-reported preferences (Kenning and Linzmajer, 2011). Given the influential power of emotions, understanding and leveraging emotional triggers can be valuable for your product's success.

Identify the primary emotional drivers for your product

As a product manager, your first mission is to understand which emotional triggers are the most relevant to your target customers and how your product addresses their emotional needs. For example, consider a luxury car's primary emotional driver might be status, while a smartphone's emotional driver might be the feeling of staying connected or being up-to-date with the latest technology.

Conduct focus groups or online surveys to uncover the primary emotional drivers behind your product's appeal. Seek to understand if customers value your product out of fear (avoidance system) or desire (approach system). Consider emotions like joy, trust, surprise, fear, sadness, anger, and anticipation in your analysis. By identifying these drivers, you can design marketing strategies that amplify the desired emotions, making your product more appealing and increasing the likelihood of purchase.

Create emotionally charged content that resonates with your target audience

Once you have a firm grasp on the emotional drivers connected to your product, it's time to design content that activates those specific emotions in the minds of your audience. This can include narrative storytelling, vivid imagery, or persuasive language that evokes the desired emotion.

For example, if your product is designed to help people feel safe (avoidance system), your marketing strategies could showcase testimonials of people who have found comfort in using your product during turbulent times. Alternatively, if your product incites the feeling of excitement and adventure (approach system), consider using action-packed storytelling and striking visuals that take your audience on an emotional journey.

The key here is creating emotionally charged content that not only informs your audience but also allows them to experience these emotions viscerally. By activating their approach or avoidance systems, you'92ll influence their decision-making process and entice them towards your product.

In conclusion, neuromarketing and emotional triggers can help you better understand the psychological drivers behind purchasing decisions. By leveraging this knowledge, you can make your product more enticing and easily resonate with your target audience. Recognizing the emotional needs of your customers and designing strategies to fulfill them will provide you with a competitive edge and contribute to the overall success of your product.

13.3 Utilizing academic research in product development

In our pursuit of becoming stronger product managers, we must acknowledge the wealth that lies in academic research. Academic research not only holds the potential to provide us with new ideas for product development, but it also helps us become better decision-makers, based on evidence rather than speculation or hunches.

Why look at academic research? It has been shown that companies that actively invest in industry-specific academic research are 80% more likely to have higher R&D productivity (Cohen, Nelson, & Walsh, 2002). In this section we will uncover ways to mine these resources for insights, integrate findings into our product development strategies, and, ultimately, find the competitive edge we crave.

First, let's debunk the myth that academic research is too complex or too theoretical to be applicable to real-world product management. On the contrary, many researchers collaborate with practitioners and strive to address relevant practical problems (Gobble, 2013). The key lies in knowing where to look and how to translate research findings into actionable insights. Here are few tips to get started:

Discover the right research: The Association for Computing Machinery (ACM), IEEE, and peer-reviewed journals in your specific domain are great sources to find relevant research. Social networks like ResearchGate and Academia.edu can also help you tap into cutting-edge scientific literature.

Make connections: Reach out to prominent researchers in your domain and engage them in conversation. This can lead to deeper insights, collaborations, or advice on approaching certain challenges in product development.

Now, let's look at two deep insights that can be derived from academic research and see how these can be applied in product development:

Deep Insight 1: Better decision-making through experimentation

Taking a cue from Lean and Agile methodologies, experimentation should be an integral part of every product manager's toolkit. In their research, Thomke and Manzi (2014) strongly advocate for experimentation when making strategic product decisions. By running small, controlled, and rapid experiments, we can observe and measure the potential impact of various product features and make informed decisions about what to include or exclude.

Practical Application:

- Setting up an environment that supports rapid experimentation can help product managers maximize the potential for learning from early-stage research. As a product manager, consider the following:
- Allocate resources (budget and time) to support experimental initiatives within your team.
- Set a goal for a minimum number of experiments to be run in each planning cycle (e.g., sprint or quarter).
- Encourage a culture of structured experimentation: hypothesis formulation, data collection, analysis, and learning.

Deep Insight 2: Leveraging network effects

The concept of network effects, introduced by Katz and Shapiro (1985), suggests that the value of a product or service increases as more people use it. This concept is critical for digital products, where there's often fierce competition to gain market share.

Practical Application:

- ⬚ To utilize network effects, product managers should be designing their products with community-driven features and strategies to encourage adoption. Here are some suggestions:
- ⬚ Collaborative features: Incorporate features that facilitate user collaboration or allow them to interact with one another (e.g., social sharing, reviews, or discussion forums).
- ⬚ Incentivizing referral programs: Develop referral programs that reward existing users to invite more people onto the platform.
- ⬚ Product bundling: Consider partnering with complementary products or services to create bundled offerings that provide users with additional benefits.

In conclusion, incorporating academic research into your product development process can bring a wealth of advantages. From discovering new ideas and inspiration to gaining a more solid foundation for decision-making, academic research is a resource no product manager should ignore. Develop the habit of consistently exploring the latest research and make connections with researchers, and you'll find yourself on the path to becoming a stronger product manager.

In this section, we will explore a couple of case studies from the real world of Product Management that illustrate both successes and failures. What lessons can we learn from these examples to become a stronger product manager? Let's dig in.

Success Case Study: Slack

Slack, the popular business communication platform, was not initially designed to be the product it is today. It was born out of the ashes of a failed video game called 'Glitch' by Tiny Speck. When the game flopped, the team was left with a robust messaging tool that they used to communicate and manage their work during the game's development (Kosner, 2015). This tool became the foundation of Slack.

What can we learn from this success story? One main takeaway is the importance of adaptability in product management. The team at Slack turned their failure into a success by identifying the value in the internal tool they had built and pivoting their focus towards developing it as a standalone product.

Another interesting aspect of Slack's success, as highlighted by Eisenmann, Ries, and Dillard (2019), is their prioritization of customer feedback. They sought frequent and truthful feedback, using it to inform their decisions and iterate on their existing product. This allowed them to better understand the needs of their users and address any issues that arose.

Failure Case Study: Google Glass

Google Glass, a pioneer in smart eyewear technology, was initially released in 2013 as an "Explorer Edition" targeted at developers and tech enthusiasts. While the innovative technology generated widespread buzz and excitement, it ultimately failed to gain traction with mass consumers.

One reason for Google Glass's failure lies in its lack of a clear product-market fit (Kee, 2015). The product was overly focused on technical features without adequately addressing the needs and desires of potential customers. To add to that, Google Glass faced significant privacy concerns and social stigmas around the device's camera and recording functionalities, which made public adoption a challenge (Fox-Brewster, 2015).

What can we learn from this failure? Understanding and validating the needs of your target audience is crucial. Focusing too much on the technology without considering market dynamics, user expectations, and social implications can lead to failure. Had Google glass taken the time to understand their customer's pain points and hesitations, they could have iterated on the design and functionality to create a more palatable product for public use.

Deep Insights

Don't become attached to a single idea

As a product manager, you should remain flexible and open to new opportunities, even if they deviate from your original vision. The team behind Slack was able to pivot their efforts and use their existing assets in a new context, resulting in a highly successful product. Learn to recognize when your product is not gaining traction and be willing to change directions if necessary.

Build strong feedback loops with users

Both case studies exemplify the importance of understanding and acting on customer feedback. In Slack's case, their relentless focus on gathering and implementing customer feedback led to constant improvements and product iterations. Conversely, Google Glass's lack of market validation resulted in a product that didn't resonate with consumers. Building strong feedback loops with your users is essential to detect changing trends/flaws and continuously improve your product.

In conclusion, becoming a stronger product manager involves learning from the successes and failures of others. By seeking adaptability, validating your product-market fit, and cultivating feedback loops with your users, you can navigate the challenges of product management and increase the chances of success for your product.

13.5: The future of product management and emerging technologies

As we stand on the threshold of a new era, it is essential for product managers to grasp the evolving industry dynamics, embrace emerging technologies, and consider the potential impact and opportunities they present. So, let's take a moment to envision what the future of product management might look like in a world dominated by innovative technologies such as artificial intelligence, data analytics, and virtual reality.

The role of the product manager is expected to evolve in several ways as a result of technological advancements. Two critical areas where technology is expected to have a significant impact on product management are data-driven decision making and enhanced customer experience.

Data-driven decision making

In a world where big data is king, the ability to harness data for decision making and planning is a game-changing skill for product managers. Data analytics tools and algorithms can help managers make more accurate predictions and adapt their product strategies accordingly (Allis, 2018). This can lead to improved product performance, faster realization of business objectives, and increased customer satisfaction.

Practical advice: Don't fear the data! Embrace it by investing time in learning about the various data analysis tools available and adapting them to your specific context. Tools such as Google Analytics, Mixpanel, and Amplitude can supply you with valuable insights into user behavior, which will enable you to make informed decisions for your product roadmap. Stay abreast of new developments in data analytics and AI to stay ahead of the curve.

Deep insight: The key to harnessing data effectively is to strike the right balance between automated decision-making and human intuition. While data will steer you in the right direction, it is crucial to rely on your creativity, empathy, and understanding of human behavior to interpret the data and create a product that is loved by users.

Enhanced customer experience

Emerging technologies such as augmented reality (AR), virtual reality (VR), and the internet of things (IoT) are poised to reshape the way people interact with products (McKinsey Global Institute, 2018). Product managers need to stay informed about the latest developments in this domain, as these technologies can potentially enhance the customer experience and provide a significant competitive advantage.

Practical advice: Start by exploring how AR, VR, and IoT solutions can add value to your product. Consider their potential applications and how they can enhance the user experience to make your product more enjoyable, engaging, or efficient. Once you have identified these opportunities, set aside time and resources to develop and implement them.

Deep insight: As new technologies become increasingly popular, remember that simpler, more familiar human-computer interactions will likely continue to coexist with more advanced ones. The key is to integrate new technologies judiciously and carefully, ensuring that your product remains accessible and intuitive for a diverse range of users.

In conclusion, the future of product management is going to be profoundly impacted by the rapid developments in data, analytics, artificial intelligence, and other emerging technologies. To be a stronger product manager, it is essential to continually update your knowledge, refine your skills, and stay abreast of the innovations shaping the industry. Stay curious, be open-minded, and take calculated risks to explore new opportunities that can help your product excel in a highly competitive market. The future is now, and the future of product management is boundless.

Conclusion

Throughout this book, we have discussed several important strategies, skills, and insights that will allow you to forge a successful career in product management.

We live in an era where products and markets are becoming increasingly complex, and product managers hold the key to navigating this complex maze (Cagan, 2017). As a result, your role is essential to the sustained success of your company. So, with the knowledge you've gained in this book, it's time to put these ideas into practice and make a positive impact on the world of product management.

In this book, we explored various aspects of product management from strategic thinking, communication, prioritization, research, and collaboration that will enable you to excel in your role as a product manager. We discussed how to handle stakeholder management, gather feedback, conduct roadmap planning, and develop deep market insights. Applying the right combination of these strategies will be instrumental in your continued growth and success as a product manager.

One deep insight we have uncovered is the vital role of empathy in the discipline of product management. Great product managers possess the ability to see the world through the eyes of their users (George, Lakhani, & Puranam, 2018). This enables them to better understand the needs and pain points of their target audience, enabling them to craft better, more human-centric solutions. By deepening your empathy skills, you will be in a better position to create successful products that resonate with your customers.

Another deep insight is the importance of a data-driven approach in product management. We live in an age where data is ubiquitous, and being able to harness this vast resource to drive informed decision-making is a crucial skill (McAfee & Brynjolfsson, 2012). By leveraging data, you can make better decisions, better prioritize your features, improve your products, and ultimately achieve better results for your organization. As a product manager, you should always be looking for ways to integrate data-driven decision-making into your day-to-day work.

As we conclude our journey, I encourage you to keep improving and building your product management skills. Successful product managers never rest on their laurels; they continually seek new insights, knowledge, and strategies to stay ahead of the curve. You must remain adaptable and agile in the face of changes in the market, technology, and user needs.

In the words of Carol Dweck, a pioneer in the field of motivation and growth mindset, "Through hard work, good strategies, and help from others, you can keep growing and learning throughout your life" (Dweck, 2008). By embracing this growth mindset, you will continually evolve your abilities and achieve your full potential as a product manager.

With the tools, knowledge, and expertise presented in this book, you are now primed to join the ranks of exceptional product managers. As you apply these learnings to your own work, you'll be able to facilitate better alignment between your company's vision and the needs of your customers, ultimately leading to more successful products and experiences for all involved.

Remember, the journey to becoming a stronger product manager is never truly complete. With a commitment to ongoing improvement and the strategies outlined herein, you will undoubtedly set yourself apart and truly excel in your craft. I look forward to watching your accomplishments unfold in the world of product management.

14.1 Putting it All Together: Becoming a Product Manager Powerhouse

In this ever-evolving world of product management, research has shown that product managers are expected to possess a multitude of skills and competencies (Clemente and Golicic, 2021). However, it can be quite challenging to sharpen all these skills and excel in every aspect of product management. In this section, we will guide you on how to integrate this vast knowledge base, balance all the required skills, and transform yourself into a powerhouse product manager.

Mastering cross-functional collaboration and communication

Product managers are the driving force behind successful product launches (Kobori et al., 2021). To achieve that, you must learn to collaborate effectively with various teams, such as marketing, design, engineering, and others. Building strong relationships with these stakeholders and maintaining clear, concise, and consistent communication is your key to unlocking all the potential resources and input needed to make your product a success.

Insight: Remember that as a product manager, you are the "glue" that binds all these cross-functional teams together. By fostering an open, transparent, and collaborative environment, you can help your team stay aligned, focused, and committed to your product's success.

Embracing empathy in decision-making

Compassion and empathy are not just "soft skills," but they play a vital role in making well-informed decisions, especially when it comes to understanding user needs and prioritizing product features. Embracing empathy in your decision-making helps you build products that truly resonate with your target audience (Melo et al., 2019).

Insight: Develop a genuine interest and curiosity about your users and their pain points. Use this knowledge to guide your product decisions and ensure that your choices are rooted in a deep understanding of what truly matters to your users.

Cultivating a continuous learning mindset

Product management is an ever-evolving field, and as a product manager, you must be prepared to adapt to the changes and learn continuously. To excel in your role, make learning an integral part of your day-to-day activities. Be curious, ask questions, and tap into resources such as books, articles, podcasts, and online courses to stay updated with the latest trends, frameworks, and industry developments.

Insight: Identify your strengths and gaps in knowledge, then set clear learning goals to help you develop a well-rounded skill set. By consistently seeking opportunities to learn, you will become a more confident, knowledgeable, and effective product manager.

Sharpening your problem-solving skills

Effective product managers possess a strong ability to tackle complex problems and find creative solutions (Wujec and Muscat, 2012). To build this skill, you must hone your critical thinking abilities and approach problems methodically, breaking them down into smaller, manageable parts.

Insight: Embrace both data-driven and creative problem-solving techniques to tackle challenges from different angles. This balanced approach will empower you with a broader range of solutions, making you more adaptable and versatile in your role.

Balancing strategy and execution

As a product manager, you need to strike the right balance between strategic planning and hands-on execution. You must be able to set a clear vision and strategy for your product while also being capable of rolling up your sleeves to ensure the flawless delivery of that strategy.

Insight: Become comfortable with "wearing multiple hats" and owning both strategy and execution. This flexibility will make you indispensable to your organization and enable you to contribute significantly to your product's overall success.

In conclusion, becoming a product manager powerhouse requires continuous learning and skill-building, as well as cultivating a mindset that is adaptable, empathetic, and focused on problem-solving. By integrating these insights and putting in the hard work to hone your skills, you will emerge as a product management leader who consistently delivers results and drives your product towards success. Remember, the journey of becoming a stronger product manager is an ongoing one, so keep pushing yourself and embrace the challenges and opportunities that come your way.

14.2 A Summary of Key Takeaways (for Busy PMs)

As we come to the end, it's time to pause and reflect on the key insights that we have gathered to become stronger product managers. Being a product management expert, I wish to share some of the most critical lessons from my experience and by referring to relevant research papers and articles. The primary goal is to equip you with practical advice based on tried and tested approaches so that you can make the most out of your product management journey. So, let's dive into the key takeaways.

Embrace empathy and customer-centricity: One of the key differentiators between a mediocre and a strong product manager is their ability to empathize with customers and having a customer-centric approach while making decisions (Bennett, 2016). Incorporate empathy as a core value in your product management practices. Understand the pain points of your customers, focus on their needs, and ensure that your product roadmap is optimized to provide the best possible value.

Insight: Empathy and customer-centricity not only make you a better product manager but also lead to long-term success as you continuously satisfy your customers' needs.

Develop a data-driven decision-making mindset: Product managers must rely on data to make informed decisions. Guo et al. (2017) emphasize the importance of leveraging big data analytics and building a data-driven culture to improve decision-making in product management. Analyze customer feedback, user behavior, market trends, and competitor insights to make informed choices that drive growth.

Insight: A data-driven mindset helps you make informed decisions by eliminating guesswork and enhancing the overall strategic direction of your product.

Cultivate effective communication and collaboration: Product managers need to collaborate with various stakeholders, including customers, developers, designers, and executive management. This requires excellent communication skills and understanding the perspectives of others. Foster an environment of open communication, and be a bridge between the different teams working on your product (Zhao et al., 2019).

Insight: Fostering strong communication and collaboration helps in building trust, encourages creativity, and reduces conflicts among team members, crucial for a product's success.

Adopt a continuous learning attitude: Product management is constantly evolving, and to stay ahead in the game, product managers must invest time in learning new techniques, staying updated with industry trends, and improving their skillset.

Engage in professional development by attending conferences, taking online courses, and networking with fellow product managers (Zeira, 2020).

Insight: Continuous learning not only makes you more adaptable but also boosts your credibility and enhances your ability to drive innovation.

Master the art of prioritization: Product managers often face constrained resources and tight deadlines. It is essential to master prioritizing, which involves evaluating and balancing various factors, like customer value, business value, technical complexity, and market trends (Knight, 2015). Regularly reassess your priorities and align them with strategic goals.

Insight: Effective prioritization increases the likelihood of delivering high-quality products that resonate well with your target audience and generate sustainable growth.

By integrating these key takeaways into your daily product management practices, you'll witness a significant improvement in your efficiency and effectiveness. Remember that becoming a stronger product manager is an ongoing journey, and these takeaways will provide you with a robust foundation for growth and long-term success.

References and Disclaimers

References and Additional Resources

1. Accenture. (2018). Pulse Check 2018: Hyper-Relevance: Insights from the Global Consumer Pulse Research. Retrieved from https://www.accenture.com/_acnmedia/PDF-88/Accenture-Global-GCPR-Report-LR.pdf
2. Agichtein, E., Brill, E., & Dumais, S. T. (2006). Improving web search ranking by incorporating user behavior information. ACM SIGIR Forum, 40(2), 19-25.
3. Allis, D. (2018). The Product Management Triangle: A framework to balance your product in a complex, ever-changing environment. Mind the Product.
4. Alonso, O. (2018). The future of conversational search. In The Turn - Integration of Information Seeking and Retrieval in Context (pp. 211-219). Springer, Cham.
5. Andriole, S. J. (2015). How to bridge the gap between business and technology so that innovation can drive value. Strategy & Leadership, 43(2), 7-13.
6. Arnett, D. B., German, S., & Hunt, S. D. (2003). The identity salience model of relationship marketing success: The case of nonprofit marketing. Journal of Marketing, 67(2), 89-105.
7. Bennett, R. (2016). Empathy: the start of good design thinking. IDEO U. Retrieved from {field{*fldinst{HYPERLINK "https://www.ideou.com/blogs/inspiration/richard-bennett-empathy-the-start-of-good-design-thinking"}}{fldrslt ul https://www.ideou.com/blogs/inspiration/richard-bennett-empathy-the-start-of-good-design-thinking}}
8. Blank, S., & Dorf, B. (2012). The startup owner's manual: The step-by-step guide for building a great company. K&S Ranch.
9. Brown, B., & Anthony, S. D. (2011). How P&G tripled its innovation success rate. Harvard Business Review, 89(6), 64-72.
10. Brown, T. (2008). Design thinking. Harvard Business Review, 84(6), 84-92.
11. Brynjolfsson, E., Hitt, L. M., & Kim, H. (2011). Strength in Numbers: How Does Data-Driven Decisionmaking Affect Firm Performance? SSRN Electronic Journal.
12. Buchenau, M., & Fulton Suri, J. (2000). Experience Prototyping. Conference Proceedings of DIS 2000.
13. Bughin, J., Hazan, E., Labaye, E., Manyika, J., Dahlstrom, P., Wiesinger, A., & Willmott, P. (2017). Artificial intelligence: The next digital frontier? McKinsey Global Institute.
14. Cagan, M. (2008). Inspired: How to create products customers love. SVPGPress.
15. Cagan, M. (2017). Inspired: How to Create Tech Products Customers Love. Wiley.
16. Cairo, A. (2016). The Truthful Art: Data, Charts, and Maps for Communication. New Riders.
17. Chaudhary, A. (2016). The Right Release Management Metrics Help Drive Agile, Iterative Practices. InfoQ.
18. Christensen, C. M. (2012). The Innovator's Dilemma: When New Technologies Cause Great Firms to Fail. Harvard Business Review Press.
19. Chui, M., Manyika, J., & Miremadi, M. (2021). Artificial Intelligence: The Next Digital Frontier? McKinsey Global Institute. https://www.mckinsey.com/~/media/McKinsey/Industries/Technology%20Media%20and%20Telecommunications/High%20Tech/Our%20Insights/How%20artificial%20intelligence%20can%20deliver%20real%20value%20to%20companies/MGI-Artificial-Intelligence-Discussion-paper.ashx
20. Cohen, B. (2018). Prioritizing Product Features and Improvements. Silicon Valley Product Group.

21. Cohen, M. (2020). Agile Product Management. A Practical Guide for Product Managers. The Art of Product Management Series.
22. Cohen, M. (2020). The art of agile product prioritization: Techniques to optimize backlog prioritization. Product Coalition. Retrieved from https://productcoalition.com/the-art-of-agile-product-prioritization-techniques-to-optimize-backlog-prioritization-9e8e504adbb4
23. Cooper, R. G., & Edgett, S. J. (2008). Ideation for product innovation: What are the best methods? PDMA Visions Magazine, 32(1), 12-17.
24. Cooper, R. G., Edgett, S. J., & Kleinschmidt, E. J. (2001). Portfolio management for new products. Basic Books.
25. Davidsson, P., Recker, J. C., & von Briel, F. (2016). External engagement and the phased transition to a lean start-up model. In Academy of Management Proceedings (Vol. 2016, No. 1, p. 12157). Briarcliff Manor, NY 10510: Academy of Management.
26. Dingsøyr, T., Nerur, S., Balijepally, V., & Moe, N. B. (2018). A decade of agile methodologies: Towards explaining agile software development. Journal of Systems and Software, 85(6), 1213-1221.
27. Dizik, A. (2018). The Leadership Essentials. Forbes. Retrieved from {field{*fldinst{HYPERLINK "https://www.forbes.com/sites/iese/2018/01/18/the-leadership-essentials-that-most-people-forget/?sh=39a3dc4c4a69"}}{fldrslt ul https://www.forbes.com/sites/iese/2018/01/18/the-leadership-essentials-that-most-people-forget/?sh=39a3dc4c4a69}}
28. Dubinski, P. (2016). The importance of ongoing interactions in team adaptation of multiple team memberships. International Journal of Management Science and Business Administration, 2(9), 54-60.
29. Dugosh, K. L., Paulus, P. B., Roland, E. J., & Yang, H. (2000). Cognitive Stimulation in Brainstorming. Journal of Personality and Social Psychology, 79(5), 722'96735.
30. Dumas, J. S., & Redish, J. R. (1999). A practical guide to usability testing. Intellect Books.
31. Dweck, C. (2006). Mindset: the new psychology of success. Random House.
32. Dweck, C. S. (2008). Mindset: The New Psychology of Success. Ballantine Books.
33. Eisenmann, T. (2020). Why Start-Ups Fail: A New Roadmap for Entrepreneurial Success. Currency.
34. Eisenstein, B. (2016) The New Order of Product Management. Benedict Studios [online]. Available at: https://uxdesign.cc/the-new-order-of-product-management-1aaa0791867 (Accessed 10th October 2021)
35. Elliot, A. J. (2008). Handbook of approach and avoidance motivation. Psychology Press.
36. Few, S. (2009). Now You See It: Simple Visualization Techniques for Quantitative Analysis. Analytics Press.
37. Fisher, K. (2019). Unlocking the full potential of cross-functional teams. MIT Sloan Management Review.
38. Fleming, L., & Sorenson, O. (2013). Navigating the Future of Work. Harvard Business Review. Retrieved from https://hbr.org/2013/08/navigating-the-future-of-work
39. Forbes. (2018). Chatbots will become indistinguishable from humans by 2029. Retrieved from https://www.forbes.com/sites/quora/2018/11/09/in-our-hurry-to-embrace-ai-are-we-inadvertently-creating-mindlessly-discriminatory-machines/
40. Forrester Consulting (2020, September). Unconventional Wisdom: Adopt Agile Practices To Foster Stronger, More Aligned Organizations [Study]. Retrieved from https://www.servicenow.com/lpgty/form-blog/20q3-FR1-EMEA-EN-FR_Forrester%20_Adopt_Agile_Practices_Study.html
41. George, G., Lakhani, K. R., & Puranam, P. (2018). What has changed? The Impact of Covid Pandemic on the Technology & Innovation Management Research Agenda. Journal of Management Studies, 57(8), 1754-1758.
42. Goleman, D. (1998). What makes a leader? Harvard Business Review, 76, 93'96102.
43. Gratton, L., & Erickson, T. J. (2007). Eight ways to build collaborative teams. Harvard Business Review, 85(11), 100-109.

44. Guo, L., Xu, L., Huang, D., & Liao, S. S. (2017). From data to big data-driven decision making: the moderating role of absorptive capacity. Information & Management, 54(6), 810-821. {field{*fldinst{HYPERLINK "https://doi.org/10.1016/j.im.2016.11.010"}}{fldrslt ul https://doi.org/10.1016/j.im.2016.11.010}}

45. Gupta, A. (2016). Product Roadmapping: How to Prioritize Your Opportunities. Pragmatic Marketing.

46. Gupta, V. (2019). How to Build a Culture of Innovation. Forbes. Retrieved from {field{*fldinst{HYPERLINK "https://www.forbes.com/sites/forbescoachescouncil/2019/07/18/how-to-build-a-culture-of-innovation/?sh=31c2740d5f31"}}{fldrslt ul https://www.forbes.com/sites/forbescoachescouncil/2019/07/18/how-to-build-a-culture-of-innovation/?sh=31c2740d5f31}}

47. Heer, J., & Shneiderman, B. (2012). Interactive Dynamics for Visual Analysis. Queue, 10(2), 30:30-30:55.

48. Herhold, K. (2018). The power of personas in B2B marketing. Journal of Business Strategy, 39(1), 61-65.

49. Hirschberg, J., & Manning, C. D. (2015). Advances in natural language processing. Science, 349(6245), 261-266.

50. Hoena, B. (2017). Walking the talk - the importance of leadership in creating an innovation culture. Industrial Management & Data Systems, 116(6), 1044-1064.

51. Holtzblatt, K. & Beyer, H., 2013. Contextual Design: Design for Life. San Francisco: Morgan Kaufmann.

52. Houde, S., & Hill, C. (1997). What do Prototypes Prototype? In M. Helander, T. Landauer, & P. Prabhu (Eds.), Handbook of Human-Computer Interaction (2nd Edition, pp. 367–381). Elsevier Science B. V.

53. Huang, L. Y., & Lai, H. C. (2011). An investigation of critical success factors in product development. Total Quality Management & Business Excellence, 22(6), 631-648.

54. Imbens, G., & Rubin, D. (2015). Causal Inference for Statistics, Social, and Biomedical Sciences: An Introduction. Cambridge University Press.

55. Isaksen, S. G., Dorval, K. B., & Treffinger, D. J. (2011). Creative approaches to problem solving: A framework for innovation and change. Sage.

56. Jäger, J. & Kretzberg, L. (2020). Too much personalization? AI Recommender Systems, Cognitive Dissonance, and Satisfaction. Journal of Retailing and Customer Services, 53, 101745.

57. Johansson-Söderstjerna, T. & Hellström, T. (2017). The contemporary development of product management: a study of current practices and expected future developments. Journal of Product & Brand Management, 26(2), 200-212.

58. Johnston, S. (2018). Creating a hypothesis-driven product practice. Mind the Product [online]. Available at: https://www.mindtheproduct.com/creating-a-hypothesis-driven-product-practice/ (Accessed 3rd October 2021)

59. Kano, N. (1984). Attractive quality and must-be quality. Journal of the Japanese Society for Quality Control, 14(2), 39-48.

60. Kaplan, J. (2019). Artificial Intelligence: What You Need to Know About Ethics, Bias, Jobs, and Privacy. Medium.

61. Karr, D. (2019). Multivariate testing 101: A scientific method of optimizing design. Business 2 Community. Retrieved from: https://www.business2community.com/online-marketing/multivariate-testing-101-a-scientific-method-of-optimizing-design-02146661

62. Katzell, R. A., & Thompson, D. E. (1990). Work motivation: Theory and practice. American Psychologist, 45(2), 144-153.

63. Keller, K. L., 1993. Conceptualizing, Measuring, and Managing Customer-Based Brand Equity. Journal of Marketing, Volume 57, pp. 1-22.

64. Kenning, P., & Linzmajer, M. (2011). Consumer neuroscience: an overview of an emerging discipline with implications for consumer policy. Journal f'fcr Verbraucherschutz und Lebensmittelsicherheit, 6(1), 111-125.

65. Kleiner, H. S. (2020). Building a Winning Product Strategy from the KPI/OKR Level. O'Reilly Media.
66. Knight, G. (2015). Prioritising the Product Backlog. Mountain Goat Software. Retrieved from {field{*fldinst{HYPERLINK "https://www.mountaingoatsoftware.com/blog/prioritising-the-product-backlog"}}{fldrslt ul https://www.mountaingoatsoftware.com/blog/prioritising-the-product-backlog}}
67. Kohavi, R., & Thomason, B. (2017). The Surprising Power of Online Experiments: Getting the Most Out of A/B Testing. California Management Review, 59(1), 74-97.
68. Kohavi, R., Deng, A., Frasca, B., Longbotham, R., Walker, T., & Xu, Y. (2013). Trustworthy online controlled experiments: Five puzzling outcomes explained. ACM Conference on Knowledge Discovery and Data Mining (KDD), 786-794.
69. Kohavi, R., Longbotham, R., Sommerfield, D., & Henne, R. M. (2009). Controlled experiments on the web: survey and practical guide. Data Mining and Knowledge Discovery, 18(1), 140-181.
70. Kohn, N. W., & Smith, S. M. (2011). Collaborative Fixation: Effects of Others'92 Ideas on Brainstorming. Applied Cognitive Psychology, 25(3), 359'96371.
71. Kotler, P., & Armstrong, G. (2010). Principles of Marketing. Prentice Hall.
72. Lee, S. M., & Trimi, S. (2020). Innovation for Creating a Smart Future. Journal of Innovation & Knowledge, 5(1), 1-14.
73. Lehtonen, J. (2021). Product backlog management: How to prepare a work item, schedule it for production, and bring it to quality assured completion. International Journal of Quality & Reliability Management, 54(4), 26-32.
74. Leoni, L., Oppici, A., & Rossi, S. (2018). An organizational perspective in the transition from project to product management. Proceedings of the IEEE/ACM 1st International Workshop on Software Centered Systems.
75. Levy, M. & Stone, B. (2019). Artificial Intelligence and Personalization Opportunities in eCommerce. Deloitte Insights. Retrieved from https://www2.deloitte.com/insights/us/en/industry/retail-distribution/artificial-intelligence-personalization.html
76. Li, Y. (2019). The impact of disposition to privacy, website reputation and website familiarity on information privacy concerns. Decision Support Systems, 116, 97-107.
77. Liden, R. C., Wayne, S. J., Meuser, J. D., Hu, J., Wu, J., & Liao, C. (2014). Servant leadership and serving culture: Influence on individual and unit performance. Academy of Management Journal, 57(5), 1434-1452.
78. Liedtka, J., & Ogilvie, T. (2011). Designing for growth: A design thinking tool kit for managers. Columbia University Press.
79. Malmasi, S., Dras, M., & Zampieri, M. (2018). Language identification and the inherent noise in web pages. In Proceedings of the 27th International Conference on Computational Linguistics (pp. 2972-2982).
80. Markowitz, M., Rank Young, M., & Kaplan, S. (2019). Research-Driven Product Management. California Management Review, 61(2), 108–125. DOI: 10.1177/0008125618817024
81. Marr, B. (2017). Big Data in Practice: How 45 Successful Companies Used Big Data Analytics to Deliver Extraordinary Results. John Wiley & Sons.
82. Maurya, A. (2012). Running lean: Iterate from plan A to a plan that works. O'Reilly Media, Inc.
83. McAfee, A., & Brynjolfsson, E. (2012). Big Data: The Management Revolution. Harvard Business Review, 90(10), 61-68.
84. McDonald, M., & Dunbar, I. (2012). Market segmentation: How to do it and how to profit from it. John Wiley & Sons.
85. McKinsey & Company. (2017). How to create an agile organization.
86. McKinsey Global Institute. (2011). Big data: The next frontier for innovation, competition, and productivity. McKinsey & Company.
87. McKinsey Global Institute. (2018). Notes from the AI frontier: Modeling the impact of AI on the world economy. McKinsey & Company.

88. Mitchell, C. (2021). The short-term and long-term effects of personalization as a marketing tactic: A review of the literature. Journal of Marketing Analytics, 9(2), 61-72.
89. Moorthy, J., Haiyang, L., & Desai, R. (2020). Personalized Marketing: APE or ROI? Journal of Marketing Research, 57(3), 537-553.
90. Morrin, M., & Ratneshwar, S. (2003). Does it make sense to use scents to enhance brand memory?. Journal of Marketing Research, 40(1), 10-25.
91. Motta, G., Cuntigh, M., & Errichiello, L. (2019). The Role of Middle Managers in the Development of Corporate Entrepreneurship: Political and Social Astuteness. Journal of Managerial Issues, 31(1), 97'96113.
92. Neeley, T., & Garcia, R. (2021). The four behaviors that define a great product manager. Harvard Business Review. Retrieved from {field{*fldinst{HYPERLINK "https://hbr.org/2021/11/the-four-behaviors-that-define-a-great-product-manager"}}{fldrslt ul https://hbr.org/2021/11/the-four-behaviors-that-define-a-great-product-manager}}
93. Nielsen, J. (1993). Usability engineering. Morgan Kaufmann Publishers Inc.
94. Nielsen, J. (2000). Why You Only Need to Test with 5 Users. Nielsen Norman Group. Retrieved from https://www.nngroup.com/articles/why-you-only-need-to-test-with-5-users/
95. Niewöhner, P., Engesser, K., Bertram, L., & Rolfstam, M. (2019). Assessing the impact of integrating AI & digital design into new product development on firm performance. Advanced Engineering Informatics, 41, 100967.
96. Norman, D. A., & Draper, S. W. (n.d.). User centered system design: New perspectives on human-computer interaction. Hillsdale, NJ: L. Erlbaum Associates Inc.
97. O'Reilly, C. A., & Tushman, M. L. (2008). Ambidexterity as a dynamic capability: Resolving the innovator's dilemma. Research in Organizational Behavior, 28, 185-206.
98. Ojasalo, J. (2001). Managing customer expectations in professional services. Managing Service Quality: An International Journal, 11(3), 200-212.
99. Olson, J. & Bakke, G., 2001. Implementing the lead user method in a high technology firm: A longitudinal study of intentions versus actions. Journal of Product Innovation Management, Volume 18, pp. 388-395.
100. Osterwalder, A. (2011). Business Model Generation. Wiley.
101. Peelen, E., & Beltman, R. (2013). Customer Relationship Management. Pearson.
102. Peltarion. (2019). State of AI, European Edition. Retrieved from: https://www.peltarion.com/ai-report-2019
103. Perry, M. (2015). The art of critical decision making. The Great Courses.
104. Pertiller, R. (2019). Agile product development teams: The impact of agile practices on product development performance. Procedia CIRP, 84, 856-861.
105. Pfeffer, J. (2010). Power: Why Some People Have It'97and Others Don't. Harper Business.
106. Phillips, K. W. (2014). How diversity makes us smarter. Scientific American, 311(4), 42-47.
107. PwC (2020). Consumer Privacy: What are your customers telling you? Retrieved from https://www.pwc.com/us/en/services/consulting/cybersecurity/library/consumer-privacy-survey.html
108. PwC. (2018). Experience is Everything: Here's How To Get It Right. Retrieved from https://www.pwc.com/future-of-cx
109. References
110. Reill, M., & Plechinger, B. (2017). Data-driven business models [Report]. McKinsey. Retrieved from https://www.mckinsey.com/business-functions/mckinsey-digital/our-insights/data-driven_business_models
111. Reinertsen, D. G. (2009). The principles of product development flow: Second generation lean product development. Celeritas Publishing.
112. Rice, M. (2019). Quantitative vs. Qualitative Research: What's Best for Product Managers? User Interviews.

113. Ries, E. (2011). The Lean Startup: How Today's Entrepreneurs Use Continuous Innovation to Create Radically Successful Businesses. Crown Business.
114. Ries, E. (2011). The Lean Startup: How Today's Entrepreneurs Use Continuous Innovation to Create Radically Successful Businesses. Crown Publishing Group.
115. Roberts, K. & Berger, J. (2018). Epsilon Research: The power of personalization continues to grow thanks to technology advancements. Epsilon Blog. Retrieved from https://www.epsilon.com/us/blog/the-power-of-personalization-continues-to-grow/
116. Rogers, D., & Tanner, J. (2017). Reprogramming Your Customer Strategy for the Digital Age. Harvard Business Review. Retrieved from https://hbr.org/2017/04/how-adept-are-you-at-going-digital
117. Samuel, A. L. (2018). The Future of Product Management As AI Evolves. HBR Blog Network. https://hbr.org/2018/06/the-future-of-product-management-as-ai-evolves
118. Schneider, J., & Hall, J. (2011). Why Most Product Launches Fail. Harvard Business Review. Retrieved from https://hbr.org/2011/04/why-most-product-launches-fail
119. Seibert, S. E., Wang, G., & Courtright, S. H. (2011). Antecedents and consequences of psychological and team empowerment in organizations: a meta-analytic review. Journal of Applied Psychology, 96(5), 981'961003.
120. Sethi, R., Raghuram, S., Sethi, N., & Horsman, P. (2020). Resilience and Agility after Disruptions: A Complex Adaptive Systems Perspective on New Product Development. Journal of Product Innovation Management, 37(6), 711-732.
121. Sirkin, H. L., Keenan, P., & Jackson, A. (2005). The hard side of change management. Harvard business review, 83(10), 108-119.
122. Skok, M. (2013). Crafting your value proposition: An exclusive Q&A session with Michael Skok. Retrieved from https://www.mskok.com/resources/crafting-your-value-proposition/.
123. Smith, W. K., & Lewis, M. W. (2011). Towards a theory of paradox: A dynamic equilibrium model of organizing. Academy of Management Review, 36(2), 381-403.
124. Sointu, E., Elovainio, M., & Linna, A. (2009). The political jungle of nursing. Journal of Nursing Management, 17(8), 938'96947.
125. Spool, J. M. (2007). The Quiet Death of the Major Relaunch. Retrieved from https://articles.uie.com/quiet_death_major_relaunch/.
126. State of Agile. (2020). 14th Annual State of Agile Report. Retrieved from https://stateofagile.com/#ufh-i-60782134-14th-state-of-agile-report/650097
127. Suarez-Barraza, M. F., Ramis-Pujol, J., & Kerbache, L. (2012). Thoughts on kaizen and its evolution: Three different perspectives and guiding principles. International Journal of Lean Six Sigma, 3(4), 288-308.
128. Swaminathan, S. (2021). AI in Product Management: The Fear and Reality. Medium. https://towardsdatascience.com/ai-in-product-management-the-fear-and-reality-6844292ba610
129. Teresa, A., & Simon, H.(2012). The new science of building great teams. Harvard Business Review, 90(4), 60-69.
130. Thompson, A.A., & Martin, F. (2010). Strategic Management: Awareness & Change (6th ed.). Cengage Learning.
131. Tontini, G. (2017). Integrating the Kano Model and servqual to improve the fit between hotel services and consumer needs. Total Quality Management & Business Excellence, 28(3-4), 347-365.
132. Ulwick, A. W. (2005). What customers want: Using outcome-driven innovation to create breakthrough products and services. McGraw-Hill.
133. Ulwick, A. W., & Bettencourt, L. A. (2008). Giving customers a fair hearing. MIT Sloan Management Review, 49(3), 62-68.
134. VersionOne (2017). 11th annual state of agile report. Retrieved from https://explore.versionone.com/state-of-agile/versionone-11th-annual-state-of-agile-report-2
135. Ward, J. (2018). Mixpanel vs Google Analytics: The 2018 Guide. Clearcode Blog. Retrieved from https://clearcode.cc/blog/mixpanel-vs-google-analytics/

136. Wilson, D. (2013). Multivariate testing in action: five simple steps to increase conversion rates. Sesame Communications. Retrieved from: https://www.slideshare.net/sesamecommunicatio...

137. Zeira, L. (2020). Continuous Learning in Product Management. Product School. Retrieved from {field{*fldinst{HYPERLINK "https://productschool.com/blog/product-management-2/pdcs-as-a-pm/"}}{fldrslt ul https://productschool.com/blog/product-management-2/pdcs-as-a-pm/}}

138. Zhao, Y., Lu, C.P., & Zhang, L. (2019). Communication and collaboration management in large-scale agile development: a bibliographic review. IEEE Access, 7, 60972-60983. {field{*fldinst{HYPERLINK "https://doi.org/10.1109/ACCESS.2019.2916716"}}{fldrslt ul https://doi.org/10.1109/ACCESS.2019.2916716}}}

Content Disclaimer:

We use content-generating tools for creating this book and source a large amount of the material from text-generation tools. We make financial material and data available through our Services. In order to do so we rely on a variety of sources to gather this information. We believe these to be reliable, credible, and accurate sources. However, there may be times when the information is incorrect.

WE MAKE NO CLAIMS OR REPRESENTATIONS AS TO THE ACCURACY, COMPLETENESS, OR TRUTH OF ANY MATERIAL CONTAINED ON OUR book. NOR WILL WE BE LIABLE FOR ANY ERRORS INACCURACIES OR OMISSIONS, AND SPECIFICALLY DISCLAIMS ANY IMPLIED WARRANTIES OR MERCHANTABILITY OR FITNESS FOR ANY PARTICULAR PURPOSE AND SHALL IN NO EVENT BE LIABLE FOR ANY LOSS OF PROFIT OR ANY OTHER COMMERCIAL OR PROPERTY DAMAGE, INCLUDING BUT NOT LIMITED TO SPECIAL, INCIDENTAL, CONSEQUENTIAL, OR OTHER DAMAGES; OR FOR DELAYS IN THE CONTENT OR TRANSMISSION OF THE DATA ON OUR book, OR THAT THE BOOK WILL ALWAYS BE AVAILABLE.

In addition to the above, it is important to note that language models like ChatGPT are based on deep learning techniques and have been trained on vast amounts of text data to generate human-like text. This text data includes a variety of sources such as books, articles, websites, and much more. This training process allows the model to learn patterns and relationships within the text and generate outputs that are coherent and contextually appropriate.

Language models like ChatGPT can be used in a variety of applications, including but not limited to, customer service, content creation, and language translation. In customer service, for example, language models can be used to answer customer inquiries quickly and accurately, freeing up human agents to handle more complex tasks. In content creation, language models can be used to generate articles, summaries, and captions, saving time and effort for content creators. In language translation, language models can assist in translating text from one language to another with high accuracy, helping to break down language barriers.

It's important to keep in mind, however, that while language models have made great strides in generating human-like text, they are not perfect. There are still limitations to the model's understanding of the context and meaning of the text, and it may generate outputs that are incorrect or offensive. As such, it's important to use language models with caution and always verify the accuracy of the outputs generated by the model.

Financial Disclaimer

This book is dedicated to helping you understand the world of online investing, removing any fears you may have about getting started and helping you choose good investments. Our goal is to help you take control of your financial well-being by delivering a solid financial education and responsible investing strategies. However, the information contained on this book and in our services is for general information and educational purposes only. It is not intended as a substitute for legal, commercial and/or financial advice from a licensed professional. The business of online investing is a complicated matter that requires serious financial due diligence for each investment in order to be successful. You are strongly advised to seek the services of qualified, competent professionals prior to engaging in any investment that may impact you finances. This information is provided by this book, including how it was made, collectively referred to as the "Services."

Be Careful With Your Money. Only use strategies that you both understand the potential risks of and are comfortable taking. It is your responsibility to invest wisely and to safeguard your personal and financial information.

We believe we have a great community of investors looking to achieve and help each other achieve financial success through investing. Accordingly we encourage people to comment on our blog and possibly in the future our forum. Many people will contribute in this matter, however, there will be times when people provide misleading, deceptive or incorrect information, unintentionally or otherwise.

You should NEVER rely upon any information or opinions you read on this book, or any book that we may link to. The information you read here and in our services should be used as a launching point for your OWN RESEARCH into various companies and investing strategies so that you can make an informed decision about where and how to invest your money.

WE DO NOT GUARANTEE THE VERACITY, RELIABILITY OR COMPLETENESS OF ANY INFORMATION PROVIDED IN THE COMMENTS, FORUM OR OTHER PUBLIC AREAS OF THE book OR IN ANY HYPERLINK APPEARING ON OUR book.

Our Services are provided to help you to understand how to make good investment and personal financial decisions for yourself. You are solely responsible for the investment decisions you make. We will not be responsible for any errors or omissions on the book including in articles or postings, for hyperlinks embedded in messages, or for any results obtained from the use of such information. Nor, will we be liable for any loss or damage, including consequential damages, if any, caused

by a reader's reliance on any information obtained through the use of our Services. Please do not use our book If you do not accept self-responsibility for your actions.

The U.S. Securities and Exchange Commission, (SEC), has published additional information on Cyberfraud to help you recognize and combat it effectively. You can also get additional help about online investment schemes and how to avoid them at the following books:http://www.sec.gov and http://www.finra.org, and http://www.nasaa.org these are each organizations set-up to help protect online investors.

If you choose ignore our advice and do not do independent research of the various industries, companies, and stocks, you intend to invest in and rely solely on information, "tips," or opinions found on our book – you agree that you have made a conscious, personal decision of your own free will and will not try to hold us responsible for the results thereof under any circumstance. The Services offered herein is not for the purpose of acting as your personal investment advisor. We do not know all the relevant facts about you and/or your individual needs, and we do not represent or claim that any of our Services are suitable for your needs. You should seek a registered investment advisor if you are looking for personalized advice.

Links to Other Sites. You will also be able to link to other books from time to time, through our Site. We do not have any control over the content or actions of the books we link to and will not be liable for anything that occurs in connection with the use of such books. The inclusion of any links, unless otherwise expressly stated, should not be seen as an endorsement or recommendation of that book or the views expressed therein. You, and only you, are responsible for doing your own due diligence on any book prior to doing any business with them.

Liability Disclaimers and Limitations: Under no circumstances, including but not limited to negligence, will we, nor our partners if any, or any of our affiliates, be held responsible or liable, directly or indirectly, for any loss or damage, whatsoever arising out of, or in connection with, the use of our Services, including without limitation, direct, indirect, consequential, unexpected, special, exemplary or other damages that may result, including but not limited to economic loss, injury, illness or death or any other type of loss or damage, or unexpected or adverse reactions to suggestions contained herein or otherwise caused or alleged to have been caused to you in connection with your use of any advice, goods or services you receive on the Site, regardless of the source, or any other book that you may have visited via links from our book, even if advised of the possibility of such damages.

Applicable law may not allow the limitation or exclusion of liability or incidental or consequential damages (including but not limited to lost data), so the above limitation or exclusion may not apply to you. However, in no event shall the total liability to you by us for all damages, losses, and causes of action (whether in contract, tort, or otherwise) exceed the amount paid by you to us, if any, for the use of our Services, if any. And by using our Site you expressly agree not to try to hold us liable for any consequences that result based on your use of our Services or the information provided therein, at any time, or for any reason, regardless of the circumstances.

Specific Results Disclaimer. We are dedicated to helping you take control of your financial well-being through education and investment. We provide strategies, opinions, resources and other Services that are specifically designed to cut through the noise and hype to help you make better personal finance and investment decisions. However, there is no way to guarantee any strategy or technique to be 100% effective, as results will vary by individual, and the effort and commitment they make toward achieving their goal. And, unfortunately we don't know you. Therefore, in using and/or purchasing our services you expressly agree that the results you receive from the use of

www.ingramcontent.com/pod-product-compliance
Lightning Source LLC
Chambersburg PA
CBHW071555080326

40690CB00057B/2240